Heavens Above!

Lorraine Stangness

PUBLISHING

P. O. Box 6753
Wheeling, WV 26003

Acknowledgments

Special thanks to Cheryl Rosenquist, Sonora Yard Goods, Sonora, CA, and Sam Butterwick, Calgary, Alberta, for their special contributions to this book.

Also, my heartfelt thanks to Joanne Baird and Caryl Yarmchuk, Quilter's Cabin, Calgary, Alberta, and Darlene McCorrister, Darlene's Fabrics, Strathmore, Alberta, for their unfailing encouragement.

Photography by Don Bartolome, Communication Associates, Calgary, Alberta.
Graphic Design and Layout, SPPS, Fountain Valley, CA.
Printing by Boyd Press, Wheeling, WV.
Linotronic Film output by Imagination Graphics, Santa Ana, CA.

ISBN: 1-879844-10-9
First Printing, 1992.

Dedication

This book is dedicated to my husband
Gordon
and my sons
Shawn and Tyler
for all the help, patience and understanding they
have given me in the pursuit of my career.

Suggested Reading

Hargrave, Harriet. *Heirloom Machine Quilting.* Westminster, CA: Burdett Publications, 1987.

Hopkins, Mary Ellen. *Connecting Up.* Santa Monica, CA: ME Publications, 1990.

Penders, Mary Coyne. *Color and Cloth.* San Francisco, CA: The Quilt Digest Press, 1989.

McClun, Diana and Laura Nownes. *Quilts! Quilts! Quilts!!!.* San Francisco, CA: The Quilt Digest Press, 1988.

Table of Contents

Introduction

Heavens Above! It is an expression that has a myriad of meanings. It can express incredulity, frustration, wonderment, and delight. In the process of writing this book, I think I have experienced all of the feelings invoked by this little idiom.

Seriously, though, the title of this book comes from the actual meaning of the words – the sky above us. Stars have intrigued mankind since the beginning of time. Quiltmakers have been using the star block in their designs for many years. What do the stars see from their prominent positions? They see this wonderful land in which we live.

Every region of our land has its own special uniqueness and charm. During the last few years, I have had the opportunity to travel to various parts of Canada and the United States, and each time have brought back with me special memories of the region and its people. "Heavens Above!" is a collection of quilts representing a few of these – the sea, the mountains, the desert, the cities and the prairies.

I like to compare the designing of a quilt to the beginning of a life. It begins with a wee little "niggle" in the back of your mind. It takes over your thoughts and makes you completely forgetful. Eight o'clock? Supper? Family? The ideas are forced to subside for a short time to attend the absolutely necessary mundane tasks that must be performed. By two in the morning, the idea has finally culminated into an awe inspiring creation that you can picture on the ceiling in your bedroom. The minutes turn into hours and finally the time has come to run to the workroom and begin the masterpiece. A quilt is born!

My first quilt in this series, *Heavens Above The Sea*, was born at a Mary Ellen Hopkins seminar. Every birth requires a little help and Mary Ellen has been my midwife. Her seminars and lectures are instructive, constructive, innovating and most of all inspiring! It is thanks to her speedy techniques and unfailing encouragement that I was able to create this collection of quilts.

About the Quilts

Don't let the look of these quilts fool you! They are easier to make than they look but when you are finished and your non-quilting friends are admiring your quilt – don't tell them that.

The "Heavens Above!" quilt collection gives you a number of choices. There are two sky variations from which to choose. The placement of the stars and the background fabrics create the difference between the two. Either of these sky variations will work with any of the five lower scenes. You will find diagrams of each of the quilts as a whole and separate diagrams of each component section of the skies and scenes. The diagrams of the sections are accompanied by explicit cutting and piecing charts.

The Accessory Chapter immediately following the quilts is devoted to small projects intended to coordinate with your quilt. These include a number of ideas for using the concepts in this book but you may want to let your own creativity show through and plan your own design using the patterns in "Heavens Above!"

Read through the general instructions carefully before beginning the quilt or accessory project. Cut and sew carefully and accurately and you shouldn't have any trouble creating a wonderful new quilt. Most importantly – relax, enjoy and have fun!

Part One

Color Choices

Fabric Selection

General Instructions

Fabric selection, for most of us, is a difficult and worrisome step in the process of quiltmaking. There are many well written, informative and inspiring books on the market to aid us in this most arduous task.

Many times I do not have a good reason or a perfect formula for why I choose a certain fabric. Some fabric decisions come from the process of trial and error and some come from within – I just know it's right and that it will do what I want it to do.

Below you will find a list of some of the terms that I reference when making fabric choices.

Value. This refers to the lightness or darkness of a fabric.

The quilts in this book rely more on value choices than on color choices because they are pictorial. The shading of the fabric makes them look more dimensional.

Stack some fabrics together on a table and stand back from them and squint your eyes. Look for the value – are they different or do they all look the same value? There must be a lightness or darkness to them.

Relative. What is a dark, a light, or a medium fabric? It is all relative to the other fabrics in the quilt.

Put a pink fabric next to a black fabric and the pink becomes the lighter value.

Now add a white fabric to the pile and pink becomes a medium, the white is the light and the black is the dark. A fabric can be more than one value relative to what is placed next to it.

Scale. This term refers to the size of the pattern on the fabric. The selection of fabric scales is enormous. They can range from tiny dots to large cabbage roses or to abstract, uneven prints. Using a variety of scales in fabric selection will give a quilt more interest.

Fabric choices for "Heavens Above!". First you must decide what "overall look" you want to achieve in each section of the quilt.

Sky – Will it be a daylight sky, a night sky, sunrise or sunset; light blues, dark blues, black, pinks, mauves or peaches?

Mountain Scene – Will it be fall or winter, summer or spring; white, brown, grey, green, gold?

Sea Scene – Will it be calm or stormy; green, turquoise or blue?

Desert Scene – Will it be very dry or will it be just after a rare rain; browns, tans, rusts, oranges and maybe just a little green.

Prairie Scene – Will it be during seeding or harvest; farmland or ranchland; yellows, golds, browns, greens or reds?

Each quilt has two sections – the sky and the scene. The sky requires five or six background fabrics and the scene requires four or five background fabrics. These fabrics should range from light to very dark. Lights come forward and darks recede, therefore the lighter foreground will seem closer than the darker background.

Background and Scene. I try to choose tone on tone fabrics for the background. Larger prints with more variance in color and scale seem more appropriate for the objects in the scene and the stars in the sky.

Twinkling and Luminous Stars. To achieve this look I use two different fabrics for the stars – one lighter and brighter than the other. Use this lighter fabric in the center and the darker fabric for the star points and you will achieve twinkling and luminous stars. Look at the color photos of the quilts. Some of the stars are pieced using this technique and some of them are not. Can you see that some of the stars look more twinkling and luminous than others?

Buildings. Use a wide variety in fabric selection to ensure the distinction in separate buildings. The sides and windows of the building should be very dark to achieve dimension.

General Instructions

Basic Supplies. We are very fortunate to have a wide variety of tools and aids available to us which immensely assist in cutting and sewing accurately. I have provided a list of supplies that I use in my quiltmaking:

> Self-healing Cutting Mat
> Rotary Cutter
> Template Ruler (12" and 24")
> Small Scissors or Thread Snips
> Sewing Machine
> Thread – light neutral for sewing light and medium fabrics; dark neutral for sewing medium and dark fabrics.
> Fabric Marker – test before using to make sure it is removable and does not bleed into your fabric.

Terminology. Quilters sometimes use words that mean something only to other quilters. Below you will find definitions for words and phrases I tend to use:

CUT A STRIP – cut along the crosswise grain of the fabric from selvage to selvage.

¼" SEAM ALLOWANCE – if you sew an exact ¼" seam allowance and press the seam allowance over, you will no longer have a ¼" because you have not allowed for the loft of the fabric when pressed. *Stitch a scant ¼" seam allowance* so that when it is pressed and the loft is allowed for, you will have an exact ¼".

PRESS OVER SEAM ALLOWANCE – press both raw edges of fabric in one direction. This makes the seam stronger than a seam allowance that is pressed open.

12

CUT SIZE – refers to the size to cut the strip or piece of fabric before stitching. The piecing charts given below each section diagram are CUT SIZE.

FINISHED SIZE – refers to the size of the piece of fabric after it is sewn into the quilt top with a ¼" seam allowance.

Fabric Grain Lines. Woven fabric has two straight grain lines. The lengthwise grain runs parallel to the selvages of the fabric and has very little give to it. The crosswise grain runs perpendicular to the selvage edges and has much more give to it. Because of the ease on the crosswise grain, it is the best choice for cutting strips for quiltmaking.

Squaring Up the Fabric. Fold the fabric in half wrong sides together, matching up the two selvage edges. If the selvages do not line up, you may have to stretch the fabric one way or the other to achieve this. See Figure 1.

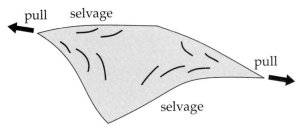

Figure 1. Squaring up the fabric.

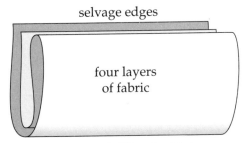

Figure 2. Folding the fabric.

After the selvages are lined up, bring the folded edges of the fabric up again to meet the selvage edges. You will now have four layers of fabric. See Figure 2.

Cutting Strips. These instructions are for a right handed person. If you are left handed, do exactly the opposite.

Place your template ruler along the right hand side of the folded fabric. Line up a horizontal line on the ruler along the double fold of the fabric and have the edges of the ruler far enough into the fabric to assure cutting the uneven edges of all four layers. Cut along the edge of the ruler with your rotary cutter. You now have a clean, square edge from which to begin measuring.

Important Rule – Square Up and Flip! To measure efficiently, you must *square up* the fabric on the right hand edge and then *flip* the fabric end so the squared edge is now on the left hand side and the selvages are still at the top, away from you. See Figure 3.

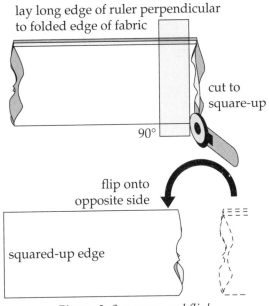

Figure 3. Square up and flip!

Lay the desired measurement of the ruler along the squared edge of the fabric (make sure to keep a horizontal line along the double fold) and cut the strip. See Figure 4.

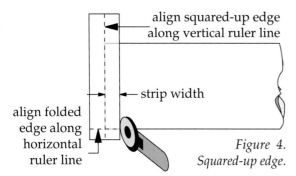

Figure 4. Squared-up edge.

Sub-cutting Squares and Rectangles. The quilts in this book use 1½", 2½", 3½", and 4½" strips. These strips will need to be sub-cut into squares and rectangles.

Cut the fabric into the required width. Cut off the selvage edges. Line up the verticle measurement and a horizontal line on your ruler to the strip and cut the required squares or rectangles. See Figure 5.

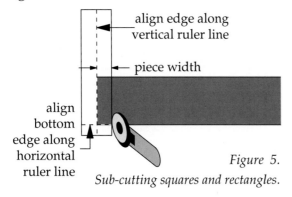

Figure 5. Sub-cutting squares and rectangles.

An Explanation of the Diagrams. There are two choices to be made. First, look at the two sky designs and choose the one you prefer. There is a difference in the placement of the stars and the selection of background fabrics. Second, choose the scene that you wish to do. Either of the skies will work with any of the scenes.

Each of the skies and each of the scenes is divided into four sections. These sections are identified on the whole quilt diagrams by heavy black lines. The different backgrounds, stars and objects in the scene are marked on the diagram with various symbols, lines or textures. At this point, sort through your fabric and decide on the placement. Draw the symbol on small pieces of paper and pin these to the appropriate fabrics so that you will remember what fabric goes where. Marking just the background fabrics is usually sufficient. Deciding on the stars and objects as you go works well. The exception to this may be the buildings in the city scene and the adobes in the desert scene. There are so many different pieces that it is easy to mix them up. Marking the fabrics will help to keep you well organized.

I am one of those impatient quilters who can't wait to see what the quilt will look like. Being persistent and sewing all the components before beginning the actual row to row construction is not something I do well. Eureka! "Heavens Above!" is the answer to my prayers! I can cut and sew a small section at a time, pin it to my design wall and admire each design section eight different times in the process of completing the quilt top!

An Explanation of the Charts. Below each diagram of the individual sections, you will find cutting and piecing charts. These charts show the cutting size of the individual pieces and their placement in each section. They are marked, as are the diagrams, with various symbols, lines or textures to designate certain fabrics.

I use a fabric covered board large enough to lay out the cut pieces for one section. This board is placed beside my cutting mat so as I cut each piece I can place it on the fabric board, positioning it according to the section chart. The size to cut the individual pieces is noted above each piece on the chart.

Rather than cut each piece individually, I like to work with strips and then sub-cut these strips into the pieces required. Look at the sections that will use the fabric you are about to cut. Are there any 4½" squares required? If there are, then cut a 4½" strip. This strip can be sub-cut into all the other sizes required. If there are no 4½" squares to cut then I would just cut a 2½" strip. Many of the pieces in the section are 1½" by ----- so I usually cut a 1½" strip of each fabric as well. The charts are there to guide you, but take a few minutes to study them and decide what size strips to cut to use your fabric most efficiently.

You will notice that some of the squares and rectangles are divided into triangle squares. For the square pieces, cut two squares – one of the first color and one of the second. Place these two squares on the fabric board in the position indicated for the triangle squares on the chart. If it is a rectangle with two triangles on the ends, first cut the rectangle (the size noted above the piece) from the fabric required. Then cut two squares the size of the small measurement noted above the piece, from the fabric required. Lay these two squares on the rectangle and place the rectangles on the fabric board in the position indicated by the chart. See mock fabric board in Figure 6.

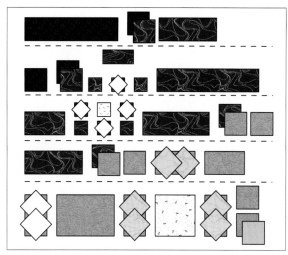

Figure 6. Layout of pieces on my fabric board.

Sewing The Sections. Take the fabric board and set it beside your sewing machine. The first step is to sew all the triangle squares and the triangle rectangles.

Triangle Squares. Lay the two cut squares right sides together and stitch across the diagonal of the squares. Trim the seam allowance of the *top square only* to ¼". Press the remaining top triangle over the cut seam allowance. You will use the uncut bottom square as the stitching guide when joining to other pieces; therefore, any shortage of the cut triangles will be within the seam allowance. See Figure 7.

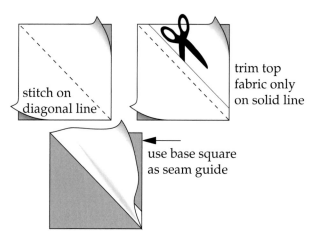

stitch on diagonal line

trim top fabric only on solid line

use base square as seam guide

Figure 7. Creating triangle squares.

15

Repeat this procedure for all the triangle squares of the section, replacing them on the fabric board as they are sewn and pressed.

Triangle Rectangles. Place one square right sides together on the end of the rectangle and stitch across the diagonal of the square. Trim the seam allowance of the top square and press over. Lay the second square right sides together on the other end of the rectangle and stitch across the diagonal of the square. Repeat the trimming and pressing procedure. See Figure 8.

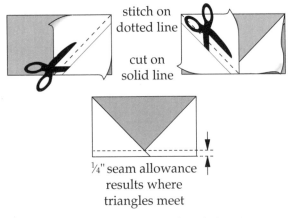

Figure 8. Corner triangle technique.

The above procedure will result in a ¼" seam allowance where the two triangles meet. Repeat for all triangle rectangles of the section, replacing them on the fabric board as they are sewn and pressed. See Figure 9.

The dotted lines on the charts indicate rows or groups. Sew the pieces of these rows or groups together, pressing the seam allowances as you go or as each grouping is completed. The pieces themselves will usually dictate which way to press. Pressing towards the darker fabric will not always apply

when sewing these sections. In some instances, though, to ensure having seam allowances of connecting rows pressed in opposite directions, you may want to press the seam allowance against the way it wants to go. One section is now complete! See Figure 10.

Quick!! Put the completed section on your design wall to admire and you're ready to begin the next section! It's so easy and so much fun that you may have trouble getting to bed on time tonight – just one more section to see what the barn is going to look like!!

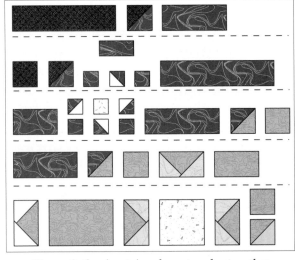

Figure 9. Sewing triangle rectangles together.

Figure 10. Layout of one section.

16

Border Application And Options. Each of the quilts in "Heavens Above!" has been bordered with a narrow accent fabric and a larger, print fabric chosen to draw upon the colors in the quilt. The narrow accent border is cut 2" wide and the wider outside border is cut 6" wide. The finished quilts then become 50" wide x 62" long. This size makes a wonderful wall hanging or looks great draped over a sofa as an accent.

If you wish to make your quilt bed size, you will need to make larger borders. A pieced border, using the stars or portions of the scenes would make an exciting border. Let your imagination go and try designing your own border by applying the techniques used in the quilt construction.

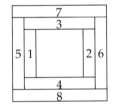

Log Cabin Style.
Measure the length of the quilt along one side, in the middle, and along the other side. Record these measurements. See Figure 11. It is very unlikely that all of these measurements will be exactly the same. For example, the length may be 47¾" at the top, 48" in the middle, and 48⅛" at the bottom. You will use the average of the three measurements which is 48". Refer to Figure 11.

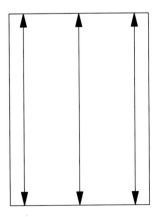

Figure 11. Lengthwise measurements.

Cut the strips for the narrow accent border 2" wide x the width of fabric. You will need five strips of fabric. Cut one of these strips in half approximately 22". Sew the two short strips to two of the long strips to form two new strips long enough for the two side borders. One 44" strip each is enough for the top and bottom borders.

Measure the strips for the sides and cut these to the exact measurement that you have recorded. Find the center of the side of the quilt and the center of the border strip; set and pin. Stitch the two sides of the quilt in this manner. Press the seam allowance towards the border.

Now measure the width of the quilt along one side, in the middle and along the other side, then record these numbers. See Figure 12.

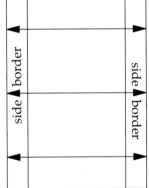

Figure 12. Crosswise measurements.

Cut your border strips the average measurement that you have recorded. Find the center of the top and bottom of the quilt and the center of the border strips and pin. Stitch the top and bottom borders to the quilt in this manner.

The second, wider border should be applied in this same manner. The strips for this border are cut 6" wide. You will again need five strips.

NOTE – When using 1½ strips for the sides of the quilt, the seams of the border WILL NOT be in the center of the side of the quilts. If you wish the seam to be in the center of the border, you will need to use eight strips of fabric.

17

Application of Borders – Mitered

Style. Measure the length and the width of the quilt in three places as in the log cabin style of border application.

Take the average of these measurements and add 18":

     Width of quilt   + 18" =
     Length of quilt   + 18" =

Cut 2" wide strips for the first accent border and 6" wide strips for the wider second border.

Stitch these together to form four sets of strips the length required by your measurements above. Stitch the joined accent strips to the joined outside border strips. You should now have four strip sets.

Remember to stagger the seams on the border strips. You do not want to have the seams on the narrow border in the same place as the seams of the wider border. See Figure 13.

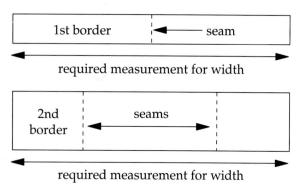

Figure 13. Creating borders.

Lay a border strip set right sides together and raw edges even on the top edge of the quilt. Leave 9" extending past both ends of the quilt. Begin stitching ¼" from the edge of the quilt and end stitching ¼" from the end of the quilt. Backstitch at both points, being careful not to stitch in further that the ¼" point. See Figure 14.

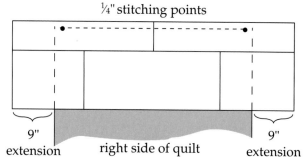

Figure 14. Placing borders.

Repeat this procedure on the bottom edge of the quilt.

Lay a border strip set right sides together and raw edges even on one side of the quilt. Leave 9" extending past both ends of the quilt. Now turn the quilt over and stitch the border strip on from the WRONG side of the quilt. By doing this you can see EXACTLY where to begin and end stitching – at the same ¼" point as for the top and bottom borders.

To Miter The Corners

– fold the quilt top right sides together on the diagonal to one corner. Line up the border strips and pin to hold. Draw a 45° angle from the ¼" stitching point to the raw edge of the border strip. See Figure 15.

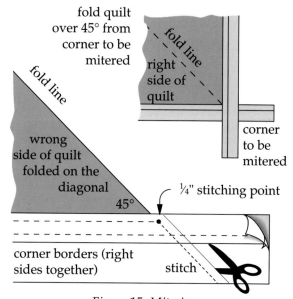

Figure 15. Mitering.

Fabric Requirements

The quilts in "Heavens Above!" use a multitude of different fabrics. It is very difficult to give an exact amount of fabric to purchase as each person's interpretation of the quilts and colors used may vary greatly. Below, I have listed general guidelines that may help you with your fabric purchases.

Stars and Scenes – for the stars and the objects in the scenes, you will need a variety of colors, values and scales. These give a good opportunity to use scraps from your fabric 'stash'. If you need to purchase fabric, I would recommend ¼ yard cuts. This will be more than you need but it will give you the ability to choose where you want to place certain fabrics. Below, I have listed the minimum number of different fabrics that I recommend for the stars and the objects in the scenes.

Stars – six to eight different fabrics.

Boats Bases – one fabric.

Sails – five to six different fabrics.

Trees – one fabric for each of the trees.

Lake – three different fabrics.

Adobes – six to seven different fabrics. One fabric for the sides of the adobes, one fabric for the windows.

Cactus – one different fabric for each cactus.

Elevator & Barn – one fabric for the front, one fabric for the sides, one fabric for the roof, one fabric for the windows and the door.

Fence – one fabric.

Buildings – fourteen different fabrics, one fabric for the sides and the roofs, one fabric for the windows.

The Scenes and Sky Background – from the diagrams, determine the number of fabrics you will require for both the sky background and the scene background. These fabrics should graduate from light to dark. I would recommend purchasing ⅓ yard or ½ yard cuts of each of these fabrics.

Borders – The first accent border is cut 2" wide. You need five strips, therefore purchase ⅓ yard. The second, wider border is cut 6" wide. You will need five strips, therefore purchase one yard.

Binding – The binding is cut 2½" wide. You will need seven strips, therefore purchase ½ yard.

Backing – The quilts are 50" x 62". So that you will have only one seam on the back you will need to purchase 3 yards.

Quilting

After completion of the quilt top, it is time to decide on where to quilt. Again, of course, this is a personal preference. The quilts pictured in this book have all been machine quilted. It was my preference to simply outline quilt the background fabrics, the stars and objects in the scene. I used a low loft polyester batting, therefore, more quilting was not required. There was no need to mark the quilt top, as all of the quilting followed the seam lines of the quilt. If you are going to do more elaborate quilting, you will need to mark the quilt before making "The Sandwich." The following list of tools and tips will help to make your machine quilting go a little more smoothly. For comprehensive information on machine quilting I recommend *Heirloom Machine Quilting*, by Harriet Hargrave.

Even Feed Foot. This foot allows all three layers of a quilt to move at the same speed when quilting. It is like having another set of feed dogs on the top of the fabric, therefore preventing the layers from shifting. Most sewing machine manufacturers have an even feed foot for their brand of machine. Pfaff is the only machine that has an even feed foot built in.

Needles. Use size 80/12. Use the best needles you can afford and a new needle for each project.

Thread. Use 100% cotton thread in the bobbin that will match the backing. For the top of the quilt, you may use either 100% cotton thread or transparent nylon thread. 100% cotton thread is preferable to polyester thread when using 100% cotton fabrics. Polyester thread is too strong and may, in time, tend to cut the fabric. Transparent nylon thread may be used if you will be doing a lot of quilting that will progress from one color to another. The smoky version is preferable to the clear.

Stitch Length. Eight to ten stitches per inch is the stitch length I tend to use.

Quilt Position. Begin quilting on one side of the quilt near the center. Roll the quilt from the bottom up and from the top down to expose only the area to be quilted. This allows the rolled portion of the quilt to fit easily between the presser foot and the main body of the machine.

Reroll the quilt as necessary as the quilting progresses.

Hand Position. Do not pull the quilt as you stitch but allow it to be fed through by the even feed foot. Place a hand on either side of the presser foot to guide the stitches and to slightly part the loft in the fabric when stitching in the ditch.

Layering
Making The Sandwich

The Backing. Assume the quilt top is 50" x 62". Remove the selvages and sew two 54" lengths of the backing together along one long side. This piece will measure approximately 54" x 88". Cut the backing, making sure the seam stays in the center of the top to a size 2" larger all around than the top, approximately 54" x 66". Press the seam allowance to one side.

The Batting. Batting choice is really a personal preference. The two types of batting I prefer and the characteristics of each are described below. The amount of quilting you wish to do, the purpose of the quilt (e.g., wallhanging vs. bed quilt) and the look you wish to achieve are all contributing factors in determining which type of batting you choose.

Cotton or Cotton/Polyester Blend. Cotton batting will shrink three to four inches when washed. If you complete the quilting and then wash the quilt, you will achieve an antique look to the quilt. If you prefer a flatter look, prewash the batting before quilting. When using this type of batting, quilting is required at intervals no further than 1" apart.

Binding Method #2

This method forms a true sewn miter on both the front and the back of the binding. I use this method to bind the quilts – it is very easy to do and gives a professional finish to the binding.

Measure the length and width of the quilted project. Cut two sets of strips the measurement plus 4" of the length, then join the two sets. Repeat this procedure for the width. NOTE – Remember to join strips with a bias join.

Fold the binding strips in half lengthwise, wrong sides together and press. Lay a binding strip right sides together and raw edges even on the top edge of the quilted project. Leave 2" extending past both ends on the quilt. Begin stitching ¼" from the edge of the quilt and end stitching ¼" from the end of the quilt. Backstitch at both points being careful not to go further than the ¼" point. Repeat this procedure with the binding on the bottom edge of the quilt. See Figure 20.

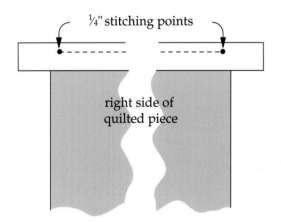

Figure 20. Binding method #2.

Lay a binding strip right sides together and raw edges even on one side of the quilted project. Leave 2" extending past the edge on both ends. Now turn the quilted project over and stitch the binding on from the WRONG side of the quilt. By doing this, you can see EXACTLY where to begin and end the stitching – at the same ¼" point as for the top and bottom binding.

Mitering the Corners. Fold the quilted project right sides together on the diagonal to one corner. Line up the right strips and pin to hold in place. Draw a 90° angle from the ¼" stitching point. See Figure 21.

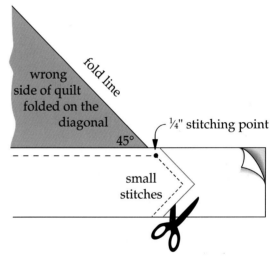

Figure 21. Mitering the corners.

Stitch along the drawn line using very small stitches and matching thread. (Be careful not to go into the quilted project further than the ¼" stitching point.) Cut the seam allowance to ¼". Turn the binding to the right side and VOILÀ! You will have a perfect miter, front and back. Hand stitch the folded edge of the binding to the wrong side of the quilt.

Heavens Above the Sea
50" x 62"

Heavens Above the Mountains
50" x 62"

Heavens Above the Mountains
50" x 62"
Cheryl Rosenquist

Heavens Above the Mountains
50" x 62"

Heavens Above the Desert
50" x 62"

Heavens Above the Prairies
50" x 62"

Heavens Above the City
50" x 62"

Accessories
Sam Butterwick

Accessories
Sam Butterwick

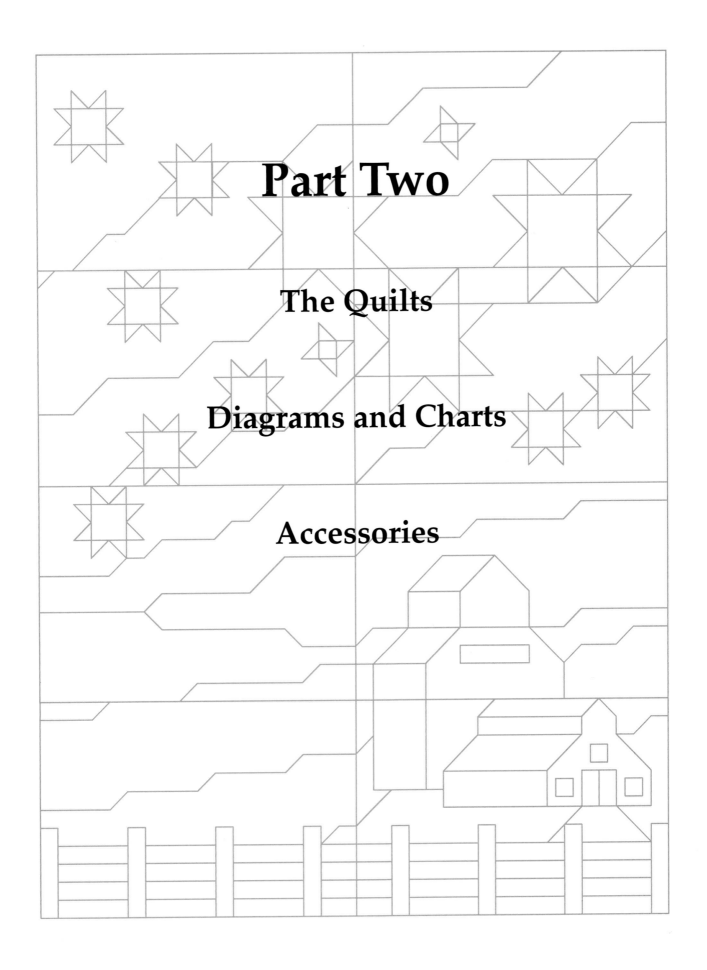

Part Two

The Quilts

Diagrams and Charts

Accessories

The Sky

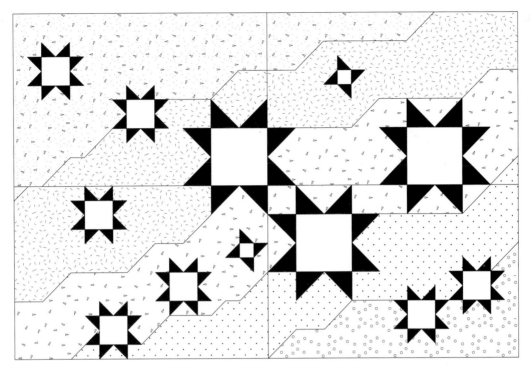

"Heavens Above!" The Skies

Above in the Heavens the stars shine so bright
Sparkling and twinkling above in the night,

What do you see from your position so high?
The earth is darkened and that is why,

The land and the people depend on your light
To guide them along on their travels at night,

From your salient home you are able to see
Across this vast land from the mountains to the sea,

The prairies, the desert and the cities below
Revel in your glory with a radiant glow.

Lorraine Stangness

The first in the series of diagrams and charts includes the two variations for the sky. The difference in the skies is the placement and arrangement of the stars and background fabrics. As mentioned previously, either of the skies will work with any of the scenes.

Before beginning any construction, read Part One of this book for information on fabric selection, color choices, and sewing techniques.

IMPORTANT NOTE: The points of the stars and any other connector corner in the diagrams are made from 1½" x 1½" cut squares or 2½" x 2½" cut squares.

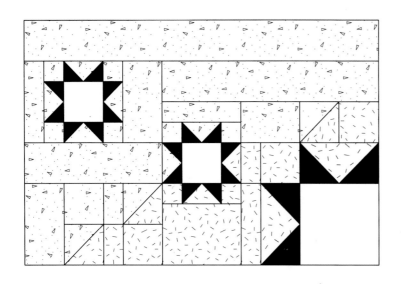

Sky One
Section One

The graphic to the left shows a finished section after sewing all the pieces together.

The diagrams below show the cut sections before stitching together. The dotted lines indicate the rows.

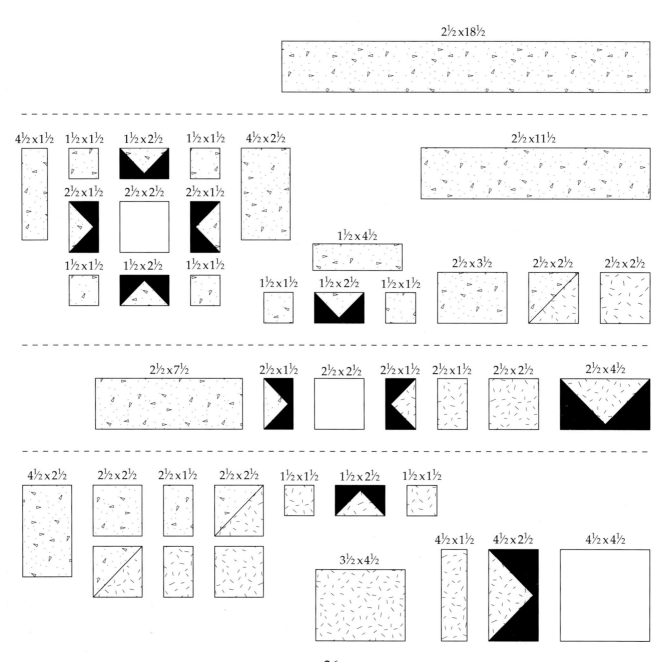

2½ x 18½

- -

4½ x1½   1½ x1½   1½ x2½   1½ x1½   4½ x 2½

2½ x1½   2½ x2½   2½ x1½

1½ x1½   1½ x2½   1½ x1½

2½ x11½

1½ x 4½

1½ x1½   1½ x2½   1½ x1½

2½ x3½   2½ x2½   2½ x2½

- -

2½ x 7½   2½ x1½   2½ x 2½   2½ x1½   2½ x1½   2½ x2½   2½ x 4½

- -

4½ x2½   2½ x2½   2½ x1½   2½ x2½   1½ x1½   1½ x2½   1½ x1½

3½ x4½   4½ x1½   4½ x2½   4½ x4½

Sky One
Section Two

The graphic to the right shows a finished section after sewing all the pieces together.

The diagrams below show the cut sections before stitching together. The dotted lines indicate the rows.

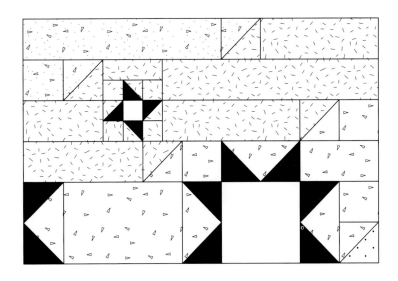

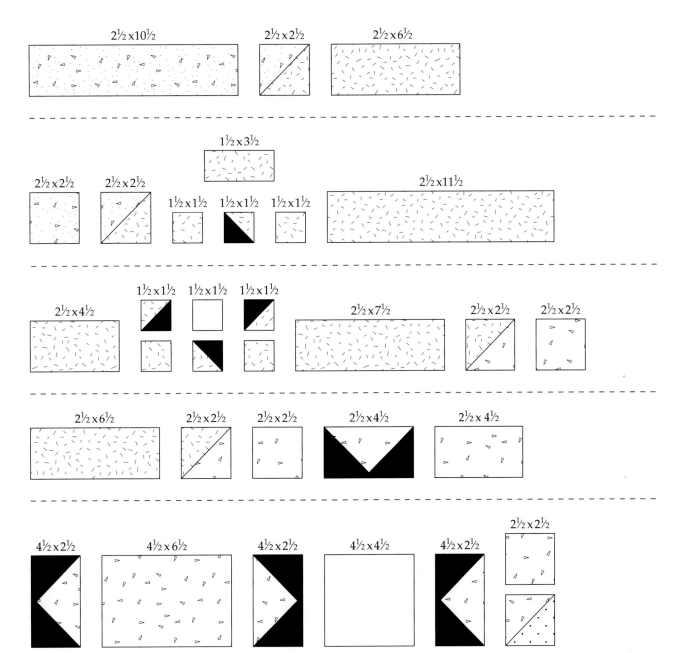

$2\frac{1}{2} \times 10\frac{1}{2}$ $2\frac{1}{2} \times 2\frac{1}{2}$ $2\frac{1}{2} \times 6\frac{1}{2}$

$1\frac{1}{2} \times 3\frac{1}{2}$

$2\frac{1}{2} \times 2\frac{1}{2}$ $2\frac{1}{2} \times 2\frac{1}{2}$ $1\frac{1}{2} \times 1\frac{1}{2}$ $1\frac{1}{2} \times 1\frac{1}{2}$ $1\frac{1}{2} \times 1\frac{1}{2}$ $2\frac{1}{2} \times 11\frac{1}{2}$

$1\frac{1}{2} \times 1\frac{1}{2}$ $1\frac{1}{2} \times 1\frac{1}{2}$ $1\frac{1}{2} \times 1\frac{1}{2}$

$2\frac{1}{2} \times 4\frac{1}{2}$ $2\frac{1}{2} \times 7\frac{1}{2}$ $2\frac{1}{2} \times 2\frac{1}{2}$ $2\frac{1}{2} \times 2\frac{1}{2}$

$2\frac{1}{2} \times 6\frac{1}{2}$ $2\frac{1}{2} \times 2\frac{1}{2}$ $2\frac{1}{2} \times 2\frac{1}{2}$ $2\frac{1}{2} \times 4\frac{1}{2}$ $2\frac{1}{2} \times 4\frac{1}{2}$

$2\frac{1}{2} \times 2\frac{1}{2}$

$4\frac{1}{2} \times 2\frac{1}{2}$ $4\frac{1}{2} \times 6\frac{1}{2}$ $4\frac{1}{2} \times 2\frac{1}{2}$ $4\frac{1}{2} \times 4\frac{1}{2}$ $4\frac{1}{2} \times 2\frac{1}{2}$

37

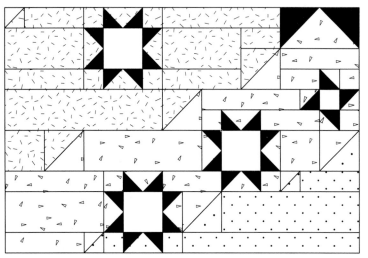

Sky One
Section Three

The graphic to the left shows a finished section after sewing all the pieces together.

The diagrams below show the cut sections before stitching together. The dotted lines indicate the rows.

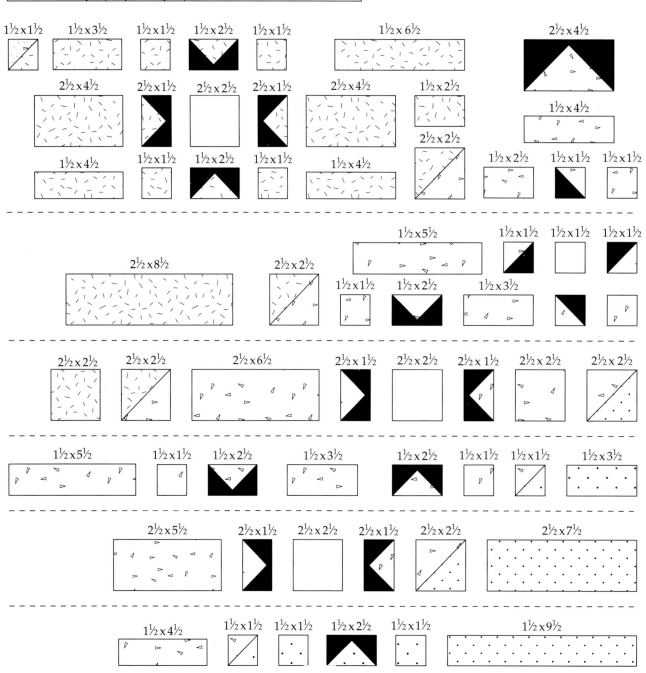

Sky One
Section Four

The graphic to the right shows a finished section after sewing all the pieces together.

The diagrams below show the cut sections before stitching together. The dotted lines indicate the rows.

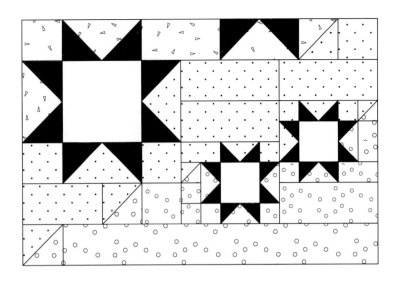

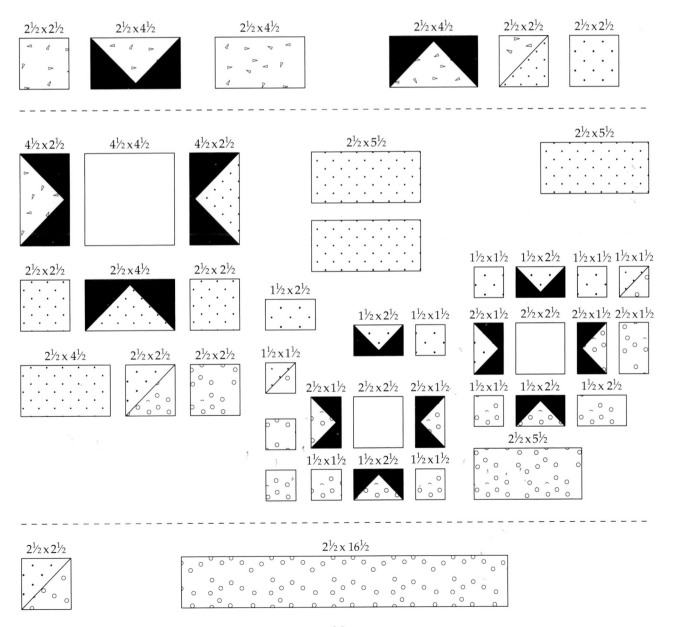

2½ x 2½ 2½ x 4½   2½ x 4½   2½ x 4½   2½ x 2½   2½ x 2½

4½ x 2½   4½ x 4½   4½ x 2½   2½ x 5½   2½ x 5½

2½ x 2½   2½ x 4½   2½ x 2½

2½ x 4½   2½ x 2½   2½ x 2½   1½ x 2½

1½ x 1½   1½ x 2½   1½ x 1½ 1½ x 1½

1½ x 2½   1½ x 1½   2½ x 1½   2½ x 2½   2½ x 1½   2½ x 1½

2½ x 1½   2½ x 2½   2½ x 1½   1½ x 1½   1½ x 2½   1½ x 2½

1½ x 1½   1½ x 2½   1½ x 1½   2½ x 5½

2½ x 2½   2½ x 16½

Sky Number One

Sky Number Two

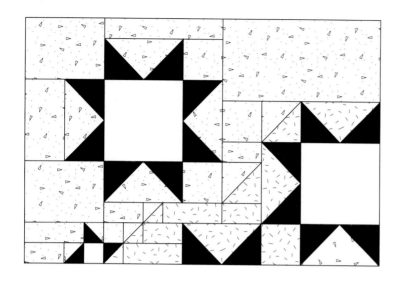

Sky Two
Section One

The graphic to the left shows a finished section after sewing all the pieces together.

The diagrams below show the cut sections before stitching together. The dotted lines indicate the rows.

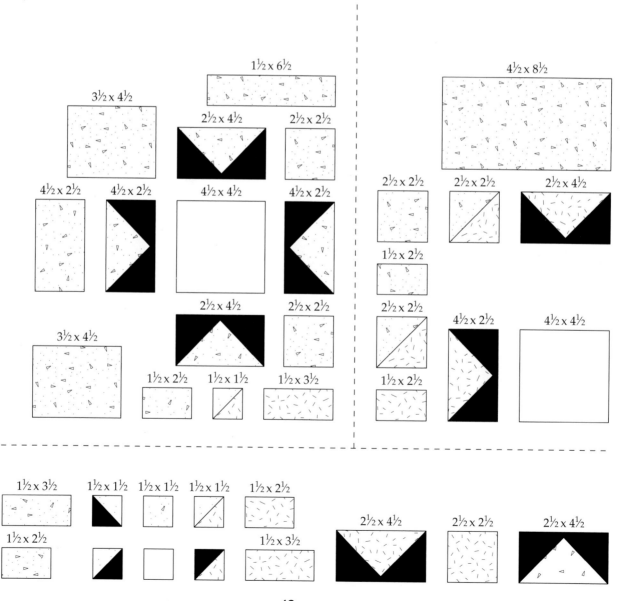

Sky Two
Section Two

The graphic to the right shows a finished section after sewing all the pieces together.

The diagrams below show the cut sections before stitching together. The dotted lines indicate the rows.

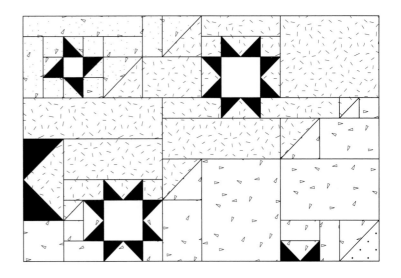

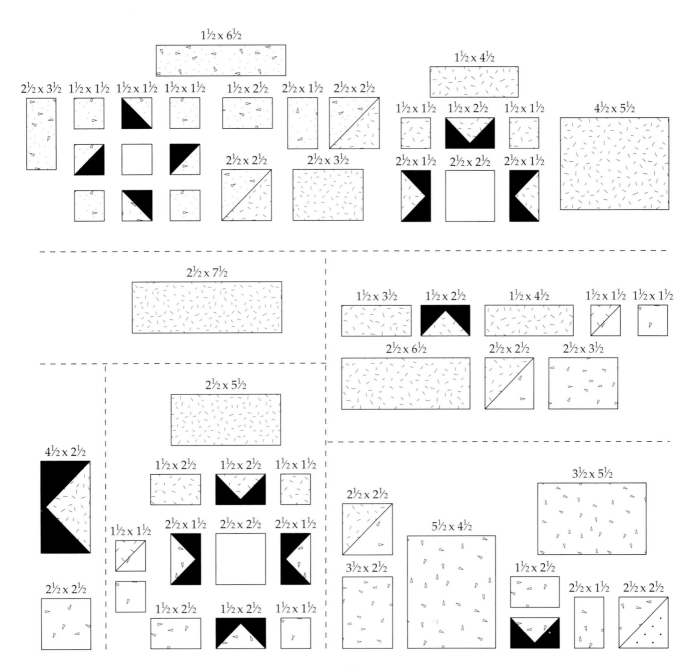

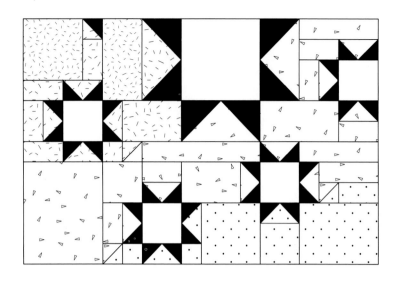

Sky Two
Section Three

The graphic to the left shows a finished section after sewing all the pieces together.

The diagrams below show the cut sections before stitching together. The dotted lines indicate the rows.

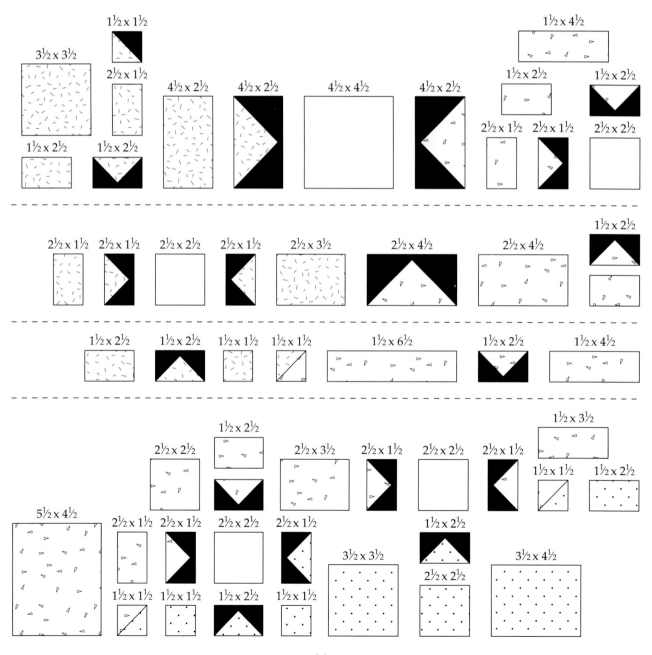

Sky Two
Section Four

The graphic to the right shows a finished section after sewing all the pieces together.

The diagrams below show the cut sections before stitching together. The dotted lines indicate the rows.

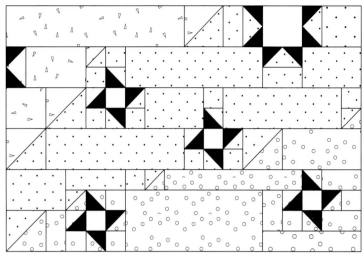

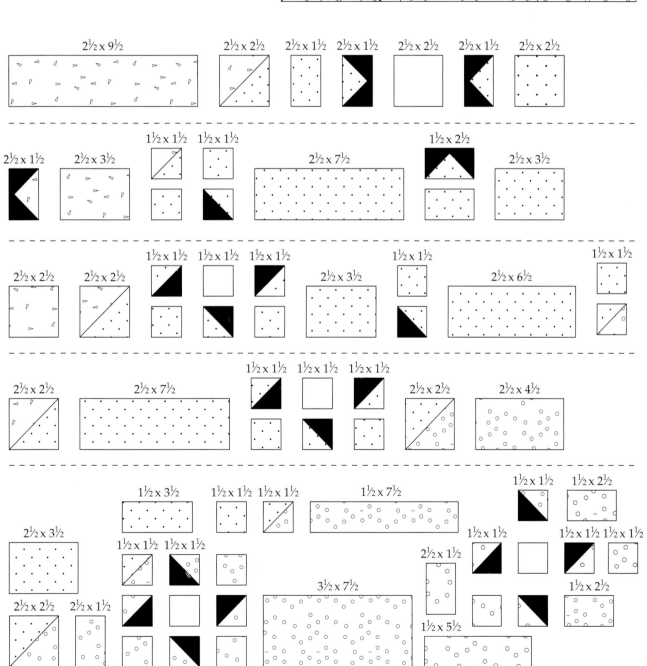

The Sea

46

The Sea

"Heavens Above!" The Sea

The sea, the lakes, the rivers, and the ponds of our world are not only beautiful to behold but are our responsibility to protect. They provide us with countless uses both for recreation and for employment. The rhythmical sound of the tide coming in, the musical lapping of the lake waters on the shore, or the evening chorus sung by creatures on the ponds can create within us a sense of well being and contentment.

The sea, unpredictable as it is, can be portrayed in this scene with a variety of moods. Choose the mood you wish to depict and make your fabric selections with this in mind.

The background fabrics of section one and section two will repeat some of the sky background fabrics as well.

Before beginning any construction, read Part One of this book for information on fabric selection, color choices and sewing techniques.

In each section of the sea layout, the graphic at the top of the page shows the section as it would look sewn together. The pieces below are the unfinished sections – with seam allowances.

IMPORTANT NOTE: The points of the sailboats and any connector corner or triangle in the diagrams are made from 1½" x 1½" cut squares or 2½" x 2½" cut squares.

The Sea
Section One

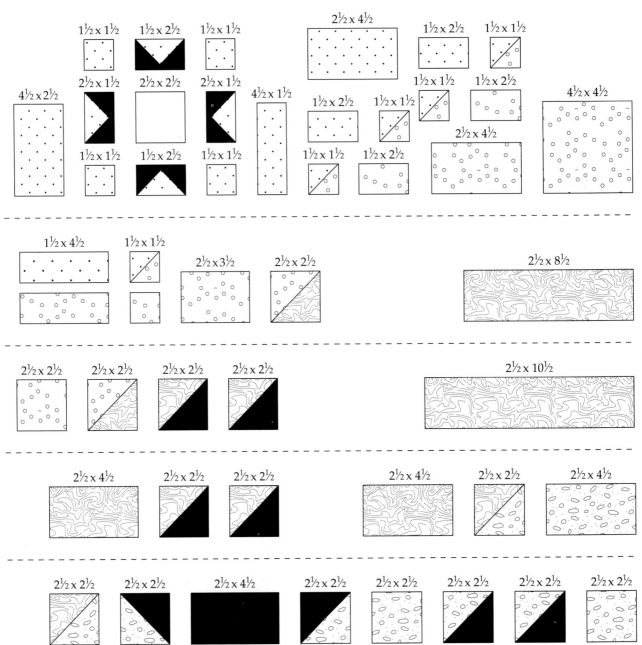

1½ x 1½ 1½ x 2½ 1½ x 1½

2½ x 4½

1½ x 2½ 1½ x 1½

4½ x 2½

2½ x 1½ 2½ x 2½ 2½ x 1½

4½ x 1½

1½ x 1½ 1½ x 2½

1½ x 1½

1½ x 2½ 1½ x 1½

2½ x 4½

4½ x 4½

1½ x 1½ 1½ x 2½ 1½ x 1½

1½ x 2½ 1½ x 1½

2½ x 4½

1½ x 4½ 1½ x 1½

2½ x 3½ 2½ x 2½

2½ x 8½

2½ x 2½ 2½ x 2½ 2½ x 2½ 2½ x 2½

2½ x 10½

2½ x 4½ 2½ x 2½ 2½ x 2½

2½ x 4½ 2½ x 2½ 2½ x 4½

2½ x 2½ 2½ x 2½ 2½ x 4½ 2½ x 2½ 2½ x 2½ 2½ x 2½ 2½ x 2½ 2½ x 2½

48

The Sea
Section Two

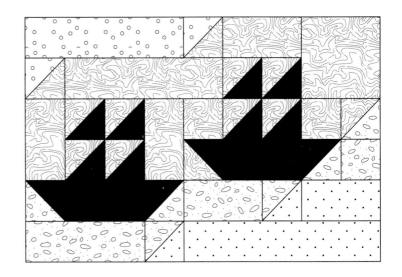

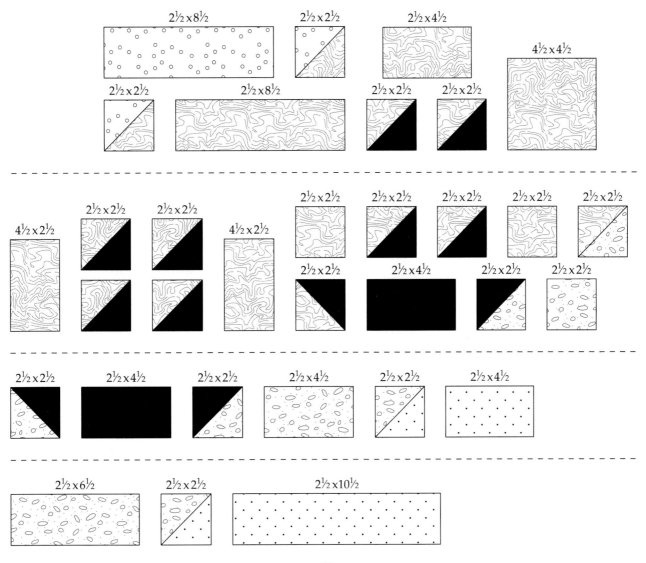

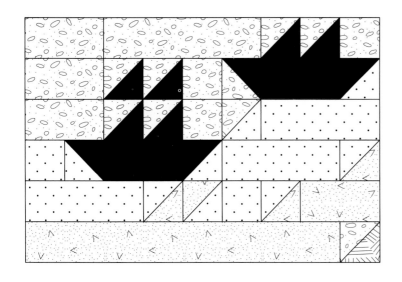

The Sea
Section Three

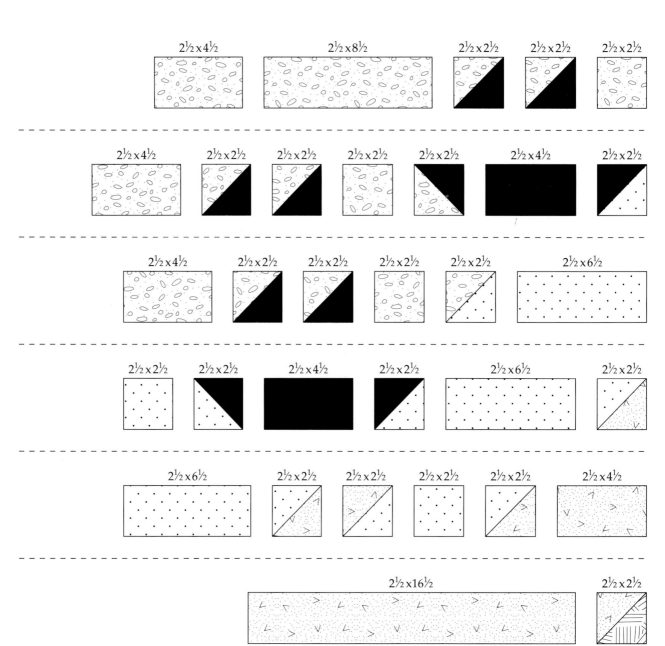

2½ x 4½ 2½ x 8½ 2½ x 2½ 2½ x 2½ 2½ x 2½

2½ x 4½ 2½ x 2½ 2½ x 2½ 2½ x 2½ 2½ x 2½ 2½ x 4½ 2½ x 2½

2½ x 4½ 2½ x 2½ 2½ x 2½ 2½ x 2½ 2½ x 2½ 2½ x 6½

2½ x 2½ 2½ x 2½ 2½ x 4½ 2½ x 2½ 2½ x 6½ 2½ x 2½

2½ x 6½ 2½ x 2½ 2½ x 2½ 2½ x 2½ 2½ x 2½ 2½ x 4½

2½ x 16½ 2½ x 2½

The Sea
Section Four

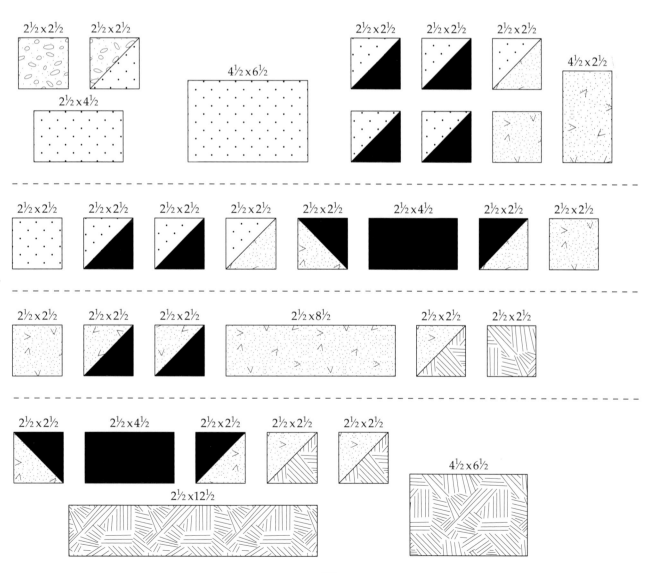

2½ x 2½   2½ x 2½

2½ x 2½   2½ x 2½   2½ x 2½

4½ x 2½

2½ x 4½

4½ x 6½

2½ x 2½   2½ x 2½   2½ x 2½   2½ x 2½   2½ x 2½   2½ x 4½   2½ x 2½   2½ x 2½

2½ x 2½   2½ x 2½   2½ x 2½   2½ x 8½   2½ x 2½   2½ x 2½

2½ x 2½   2½ x 4½   2½ x 2½   2½ x 2½   2½ x 2½   4½ x 6½

2½ x 12½

The Mountains

The Mountains

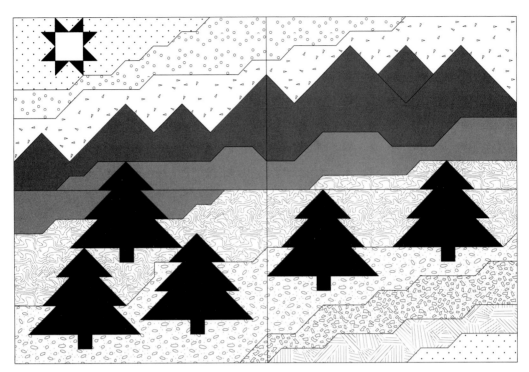

"Heavens Above!" The Mountains

What a wonder they are! Standing there, austere and foreboding yet somehow majestic in their beauty. Formed millions of years ago they are a reminder of an age so long ago it dwarfs the short existence we have on this earth.

How many wonderful holidays have I enjoyed camping in the mountains. Breathing the fresh mountain air, hiking along the moss covered trails among giant fir trees, encountering the wildlife in its natural habitat and gazing in awe at the towering peaks and craggy slopes of the mountains is an experience of joy.

Our feelings and interpretations of the mountains can be expressed using the mode all quilters use best – fabric! Have fun expressing your feelings in the "Heavens Above!" The Mountains quilt.

The background fabrics of section one and section two will repeat some of the sky background fabrics as well.

Before beginning any construction, read Part One of this book for information on

fabric selection, color choices and sewing techniques.

In each section of the mountain layout, the graphic at the top of the page shows the section as it would look sewn together. The pieces below are the unfinished sections.

IMPORTANT NOTE: The points of the trees and any connector corner in the diagrams are constructed from 1½" x 1½" cut squares or 2½" x 2½" cut squares.

The Mountains
Section One

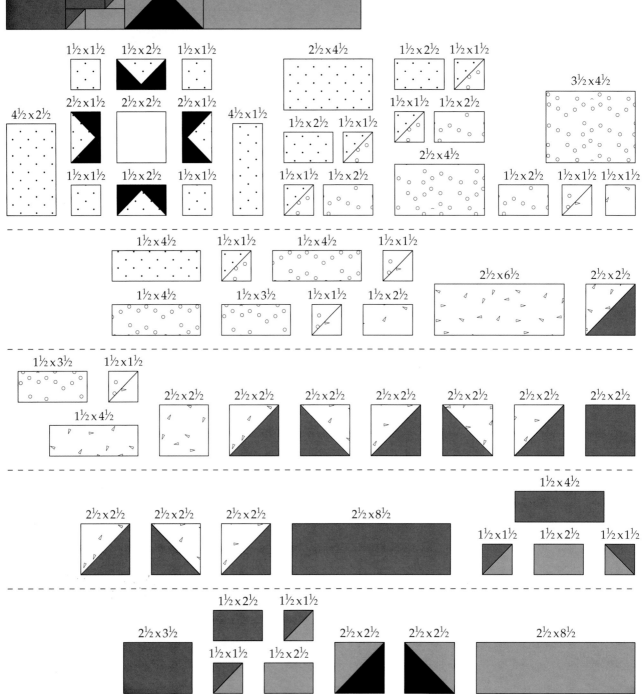

The Mountains Section Two

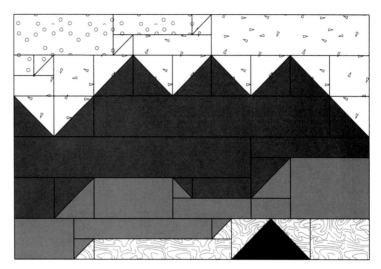

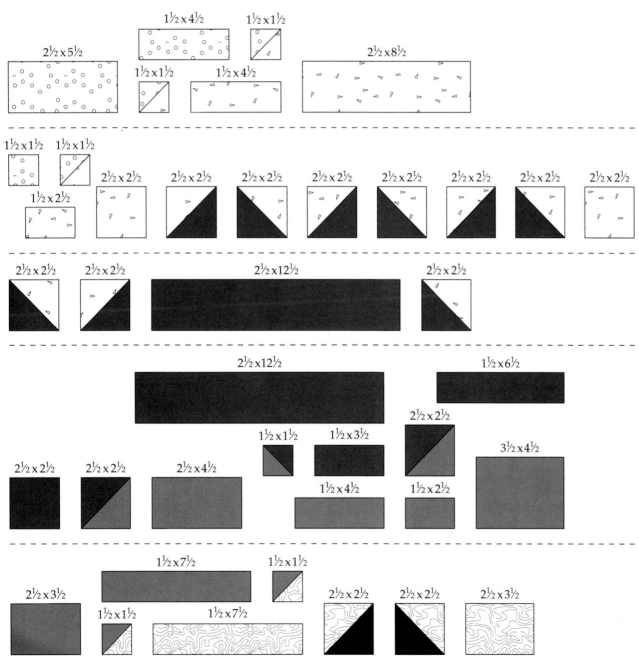

$2\frac{1}{2} \times 5\frac{1}{2}$

$1\frac{1}{2} \times 4\frac{1}{2}$ $1\frac{1}{2} \times 1\frac{1}{2}$

$1\frac{1}{2} \times 1\frac{1}{2}$ $1\frac{1}{2} \times 4\frac{1}{2}$

$2\frac{1}{2} \times 8\frac{1}{2}$

$1\frac{1}{2} \times 1\frac{1}{2}$ $1\frac{1}{2} \times 1\frac{1}{2}$

$1\frac{1}{2} \times 2\frac{1}{2}$ $2\frac{1}{2} \times 2\frac{1}{2}$ $2\frac{1}{2} \times 2\frac{1}{2}$ $2\frac{1}{2} \times 2\frac{1}{2}$ $2\frac{1}{2} \times 2\frac{1}{2}$ $2\frac{1}{2} \times 2\frac{1}{2}$ $2\frac{1}{2} \times 2\frac{1}{2}$ $2\frac{1}{2} \times 2\frac{1}{2}$ $2\frac{1}{2} \times 2\frac{1}{2}$

$2\frac{1}{2} \times 2\frac{1}{2}$ $2\frac{1}{2} \times 2\frac{1}{2}$ $2\frac{1}{2} \times 12\frac{1}{2}$ $2\frac{1}{2} \times 2\frac{1}{2}$

$2\frac{1}{2} \times 12\frac{1}{2}$ $1\frac{1}{2} \times 6\frac{1}{2}$

$2\frac{1}{2} \times 2\frac{1}{2}$

$1\frac{1}{2} \times 1\frac{1}{2}$ $1\frac{1}{2} \times 3\frac{1}{2}$

$3\frac{1}{2} \times 4\frac{1}{2}$

$2\frac{1}{2} \times 2\frac{1}{2}$ $2\frac{1}{2} \times 2\frac{1}{2}$ $2\frac{1}{2} \times 4\frac{1}{2}$ $1\frac{1}{2} \times 4\frac{1}{2}$ $1\frac{1}{2} \times 2\frac{1}{2}$

$1\frac{1}{2} \times 7\frac{1}{2}$ $1\frac{1}{2} \times 1\frac{1}{2}$

$2\frac{1}{2} \times 3\frac{1}{2}$ $1\frac{1}{2} \times 1\frac{1}{2}$ $1\frac{1}{2} \times 7\frac{1}{2}$ $2\frac{1}{2} \times 2\frac{1}{2}$ $2\frac{1}{2} \times 2\frac{1}{2}$ $2\frac{1}{2} \times 3\frac{1}{2}$

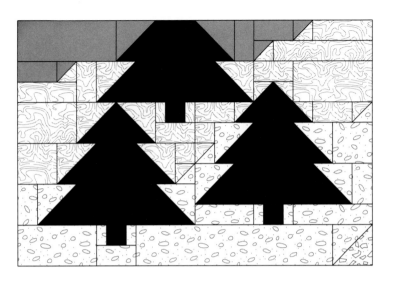

The Mountains
Section Three

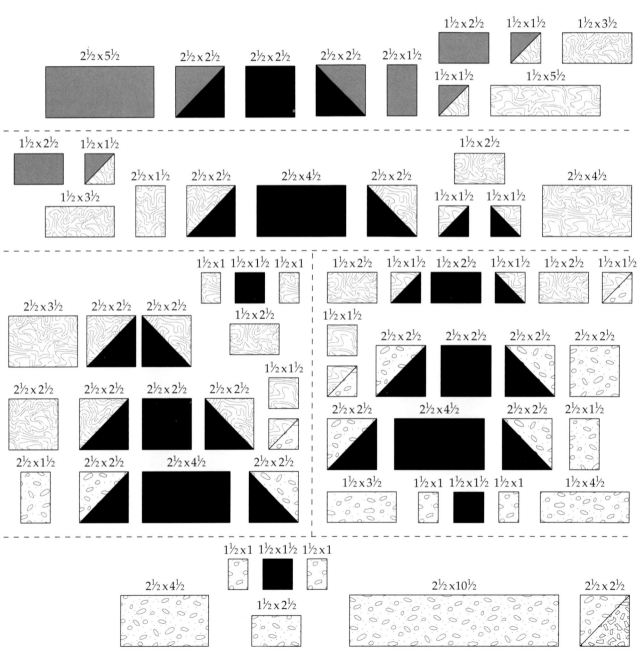

$2\frac{1}{2} \times 5\frac{1}{2}$

$2\frac{1}{2} \times 2\frac{1}{2}$

$2\frac{1}{2} \times 2\frac{1}{2}$

$2\frac{1}{2} \times 2\frac{1}{2}$

$2\frac{1}{2} \times 1\frac{1}{2}$

$1\frac{1}{2} \times 2\frac{1}{2}$

$1\frac{1}{2} \times 1\frac{1}{2}$

$1\frac{1}{2} \times 3\frac{1}{2}$

$1\frac{1}{2} \times 1\frac{1}{2}$

$1\frac{1}{2} \times 5\frac{1}{2}$

$1\frac{1}{2} \times 2\frac{1}{2}$

$1\frac{1}{2} \times 1\frac{1}{2}$

$1\frac{1}{2} \times 3\frac{1}{2}$

$2\frac{1}{2} \times 1\frac{1}{2}$

$2\frac{1}{2} \times 2\frac{1}{2}$

$2\frac{1}{2} \times 4\frac{1}{2}$

$2\frac{1}{2} \times 2\frac{1}{2}$

$1\frac{1}{2} \times 2\frac{1}{2}$

$2\frac{1}{2} \times 4\frac{1}{2}$

$1\frac{1}{2} \times 1\frac{1}{2}$

$1\frac{1}{2} \times 1\frac{1}{2}$

$1\frac{1}{2} \times 1$

$1\frac{1}{2} \times 1\frac{1}{2}$

$1\frac{1}{2} \times 1$

$1\frac{1}{2} \times 2\frac{1}{2}$

$1\frac{1}{2} \times 1\frac{1}{2}$

$1\frac{1}{2} \times 2\frac{1}{2}$

$1\frac{1}{2} \times 1\frac{1}{2}$

$1\frac{1}{2} \times 2\frac{1}{2}$

$1\frac{1}{2} \times 1\frac{1}{2}$

$2\frac{1}{2} \times 3\frac{1}{2}$

$2\frac{1}{2} \times 2\frac{1}{2}$

$2\frac{1}{2} \times 2\frac{1}{2}$

$1\frac{1}{2} \times 2\frac{1}{2}$

$1\frac{1}{2} \times 2\frac{1}{2}$

$2\frac{1}{2} \times 2\frac{1}{2}$

$2\frac{1}{2} \times 2\frac{1}{2}$

$2\frac{1}{2} \times 2\frac{1}{2}$

$2\frac{1}{2} \times 2\frac{1}{2}$

$2\frac{1}{2} \times 2\frac{1}{2}$

$2\frac{1}{2} \times 2\frac{1}{2}$

$2\frac{1}{2} \times 2\frac{1}{2}$

$2\frac{1}{2} \times 2\frac{1}{2}$

$1\frac{1}{2} \times 1\frac{1}{2}$

$2\frac{1}{2} \times 2\frac{1}{2}$

$2\frac{1}{2} \times 4\frac{1}{2}$

$2\frac{1}{2} \times 2\frac{1}{2}$

$2\frac{1}{2} \times 1\frac{1}{2}$

$2\frac{1}{2} \times 1\frac{1}{2}$

$2\frac{1}{2} \times 2\frac{1}{2}$

$2\frac{1}{2} \times 4\frac{1}{2}$

$2\frac{1}{2} \times 2\frac{1}{2}$

$1\frac{1}{2} \times 3\frac{1}{2}$

$1\frac{1}{2} \times 1$

$1\frac{1}{2} \times 1\frac{1}{2}$

$1\frac{1}{2} \times 1$

$1\frac{1}{2} \times 4\frac{1}{2}$

$1\frac{1}{2} \times 1$

$1\frac{1}{2} \times 1\frac{1}{2}$

$1\frac{1}{2} \times 1$

$2\frac{1}{2} \times 4\frac{1}{2}$

$1\frac{1}{2} \times 2\frac{1}{2}$

$2\frac{1}{2} \times 10\frac{1}{2}$

$2\frac{1}{2} \times 2\frac{1}{2}$

The Mountains
Section Four

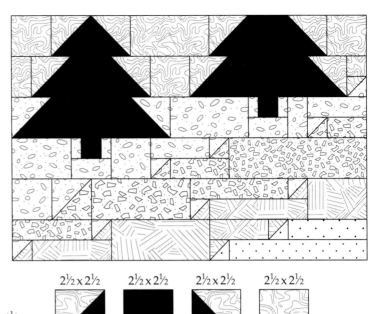

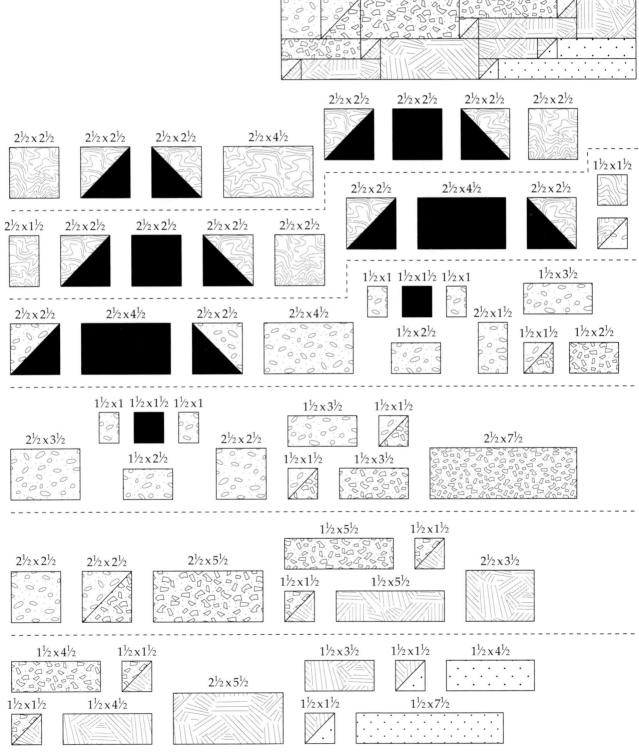

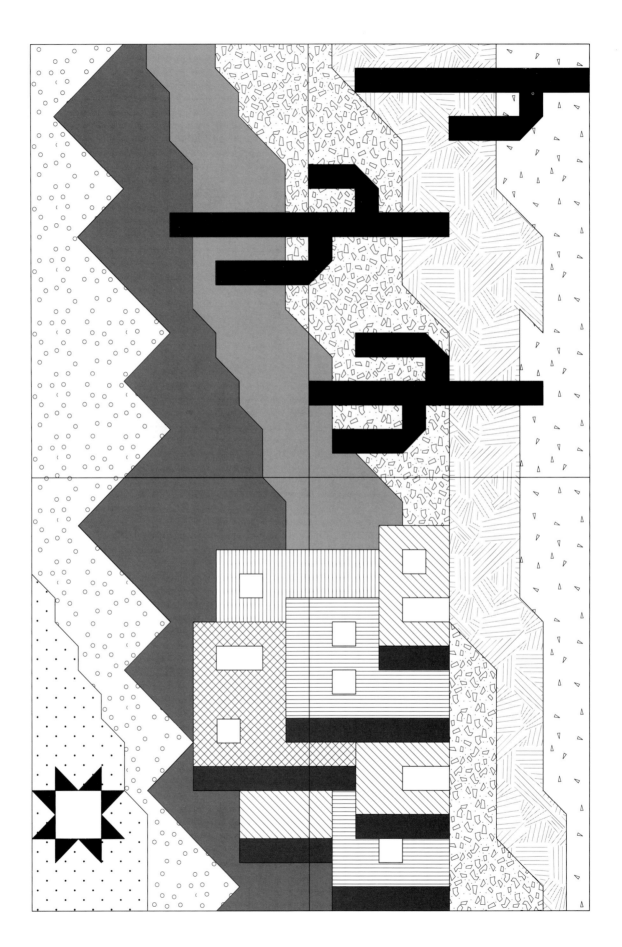

The Desert

58

The Desert

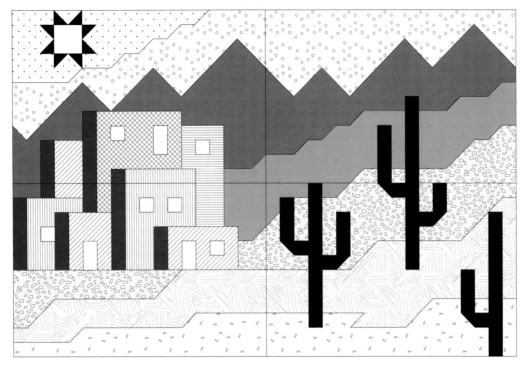

"Heavens Above!" The Desert

The winds blow the shifting sands across the never ending vastness of the desert. Birds circle in their quest for a meager fare from the land below. Amid the infinite boundaries and solitude of the desert is found an unequaled vista – the oasis. Swaying palm trees guarding over gardens of desert plants and flowers, the stoical cactus stately in its rigid stance and the mystical desert creatures scurrying about the hot dry land belies the forbidding expanses beyond. The rugged, color splashed mountains in the distance look down upon the scene below as if in awe. How beautiful the desert is!

The background fabrics of section one and section two will repeat some of the sky background fabrics as well.

Before beginning any construction, read Part One of this book for information on fabric selection, color choices and sewing techniques.

In each section of the desert layout, the graphic at the top of the page shows the section as it would look sewn together. The pieces below are the unfinished sections – with seam allowances.

IMPORTANT NOTE: Any connector corner or triangle in the desert diagrams are constructed from 1½" x 1½" cut squares or 2½" x 2½" cut squares.

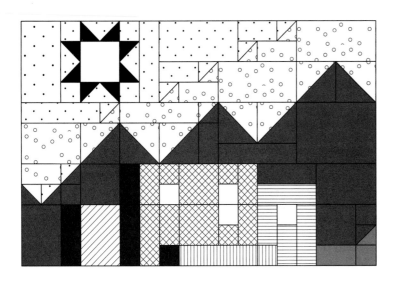

The Desert
Section One

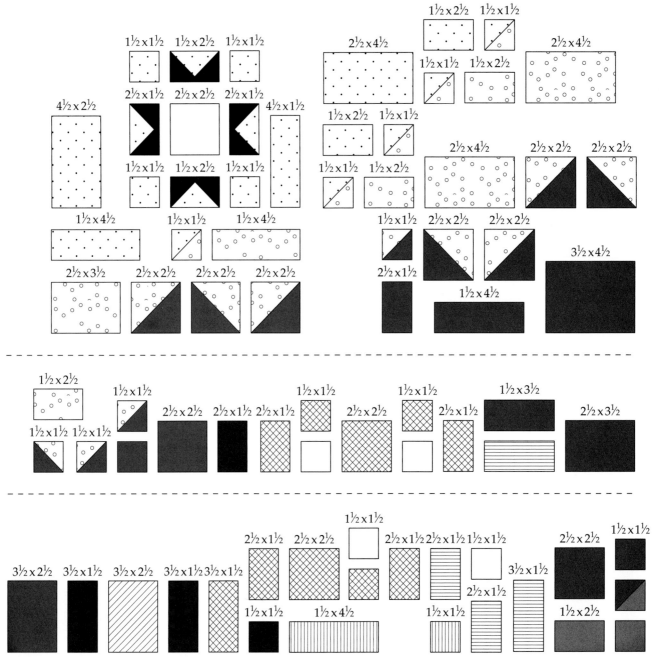

The Desert Section Two

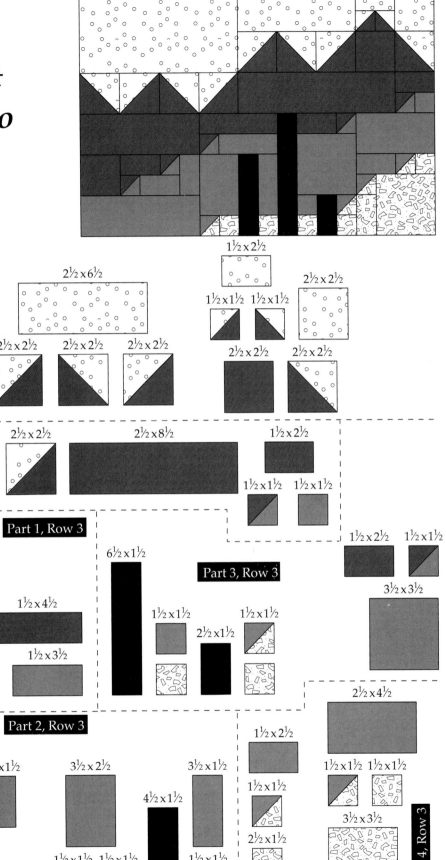

$4\frac{1}{2} \times 8\frac{1}{2}$

$2\frac{1}{2} \times 6\frac{1}{2}$

$2\frac{1}{2} \times 2\frac{1}{2}$ $2\frac{1}{2} \times 2\frac{1}{2}$ $2\frac{1}{2} \times 2\frac{1}{2}$

$1\frac{1}{2} \times 2\frac{1}{2}$

$1\frac{1}{2} \times 1\frac{1}{2}$ $1\frac{1}{2} \times 1\frac{1}{2}$ $2\frac{1}{2} \times 2\frac{1}{2}$

$2\frac{1}{2} \times 2\frac{1}{2}$ $2\frac{1}{2} \times 2\frac{1}{2}$

$2\frac{1}{2} \times 2\frac{1}{2}$ $2\frac{1}{2} \times 2\frac{1}{2}$ $2\frac{1}{2} \times 2\frac{1}{2}$ $2\frac{1}{2} \times 2\frac{1}{2}$ $2\frac{1}{2} \times 8\frac{1}{2}$ $1\frac{1}{2} \times 2\frac{1}{2}$

$1\frac{1}{2} \times 1\frac{1}{2}$ $1\frac{1}{2} \times 1\frac{1}{2}$

$1\frac{1}{2} \times 2\frac{1}{2}$ $1\frac{1}{2} \times 1\frac{1}{2}$

Part 1, Row 3	Part 3 Row 3	Part 4 Row 3
Part 2, Row 3		

Part 1, Row 3

$3\frac{1}{2} \times 3\frac{1}{2}$

$6\frac{1}{2} \times 1\frac{1}{2}$

Part 3, Row 3

$1\frac{1}{2} \times 4\frac{1}{2}$

$1\frac{1}{2} \times 1\frac{1}{2}$ $1\frac{1}{2} \times 1\frac{1}{2}$

$2\frac{1}{2} \times 6\frac{1}{2}$ $1\frac{1}{2} \times 1\frac{1}{2}$ $1\frac{1}{2} \times 3\frac{1}{2}$ $2\frac{1}{2} \times 1\frac{1}{2}$

$2\frac{1}{2} \times 4\frac{1}{2}$

$1\frac{1}{2} \times 2\frac{1}{2}$

$1\frac{1}{2} \times 1\frac{1}{2}$ $1\frac{1}{2} \times 1\frac{1}{2}$

Part 2, Row 3

$1\frac{1}{2} \times 2\frac{1}{2}$ $1\frac{1}{2} \times 1\frac{1}{2}$

$2\frac{1}{2} \times 2\frac{1}{2}$ $2\frac{1}{2} \times 1\frac{1}{2}$ $3\frac{1}{2} \times 2\frac{1}{2}$ $3\frac{1}{2} \times 1\frac{1}{2}$

$1\frac{1}{2} \times 1\frac{1}{2}$ $1\frac{1}{2} \times 2\frac{1}{2}$

$1\frac{1}{2} \times 1\frac{1}{2}$

$4\frac{1}{2} \times 1\frac{1}{2}$

$2\frac{1}{2} \times 1\frac{1}{2}$

$2\frac{1}{2} \times 6\frac{1}{2}$

$3\frac{1}{2} \times 3\frac{1}{2}$

Part 4, Row 3

$1\frac{1}{2} \times 1\frac{1}{2}$ $1\frac{1}{2} \times 1\frac{1}{2}$ $1\frac{1}{2} \times 1\frac{1}{2}$ $1\frac{1}{2} \times 1\frac{1}{2}$

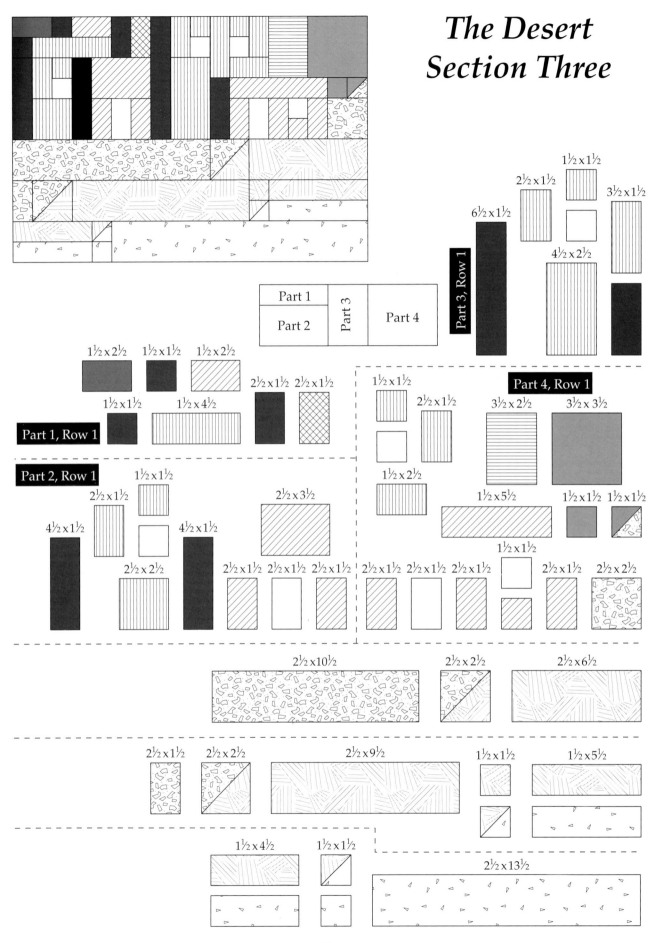

Part 1
Part 2
Part 3
Part 4

Part 3, Row 1

$6\frac{1}{2} \times 1\frac{1}{2}$

$2\frac{1}{2} \times 1\frac{1}{2}$

$1\frac{1}{2} \times 1\frac{1}{2}$

$3\frac{1}{2} \times 1\frac{1}{2}$

$4\frac{1}{2} \times 2\frac{1}{2}$

$1\frac{1}{2} \times 2\frac{1}{2}$ $1\frac{1}{2} \times 1\frac{1}{2}$ $1\frac{1}{2} \times 2\frac{1}{2}$

$2\frac{1}{2} \times 1\frac{1}{2}$ $2\frac{1}{2} \times 1\frac{1}{2}$

$1\frac{1}{2} \times 1\frac{1}{2}$ $1\frac{1}{2} \times 4\frac{1}{2}$

Part 1, Row 1

Part 4, Row 1

$1\frac{1}{2} \times 1\frac{1}{2}$

$2\frac{1}{2} \times 1\frac{1}{2}$ $3\frac{1}{2} \times 2\frac{1}{2}$ $3\frac{1}{2} \times 3\frac{1}{2}$

Part 2, Row 1

$1\frac{1}{2} \times 1\frac{1}{2}$

$2\frac{1}{2} \times 1\frac{1}{2}$

$2\frac{1}{2} \times 3\frac{1}{2}$

$1\frac{1}{2} \times 2\frac{1}{2}$

$4\frac{1}{2} \times 1\frac{1}{2}$ $4\frac{1}{2} \times 1\frac{1}{2}$

$1\frac{1}{2} \times 5\frac{1}{2}$ $1\frac{1}{2} \times 1\frac{1}{2}$ $1\frac{1}{2} \times 1\frac{1}{2}$

$1\frac{1}{2} \times 1\frac{1}{2}$

$2\frac{1}{2} \times 2\frac{1}{2}$ $2\frac{1}{2} \times 1\frac{1}{2}$ $2\frac{1}{2} \times 1\frac{1}{2}$ $2\frac{1}{2} \times 1\frac{1}{2}$ $2\frac{1}{2} \times 1\frac{1}{2}$ $2\frac{1}{2} \times 1\frac{1}{2}$ $2\frac{1}{2} \times 1\frac{1}{2}$ $2\frac{1}{2} \times 1\frac{1}{2}$ $2\frac{1}{2} \times 2\frac{1}{2}$

$2\frac{1}{2} \times 10\frac{1}{2}$ $2\frac{1}{2} \times 2\frac{1}{2}$ $2\frac{1}{2} \times 6\frac{1}{2}$

$2\frac{1}{2} \times 1\frac{1}{2}$ $2\frac{1}{2} \times 2\frac{1}{2}$ $2\frac{1}{2} \times 9\frac{1}{2}$ $1\frac{1}{2} \times 1\frac{1}{2}$ $1\frac{1}{2} \times 5\frac{1}{2}$

$1\frac{1}{2} \times 4\frac{1}{2}$ $1\frac{1}{2} \times 1\frac{1}{2}$ $2\frac{1}{2} \times 13\frac{1}{2}$

The Desert
Section Four

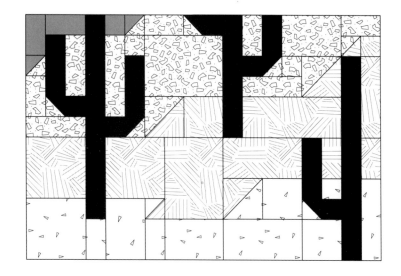

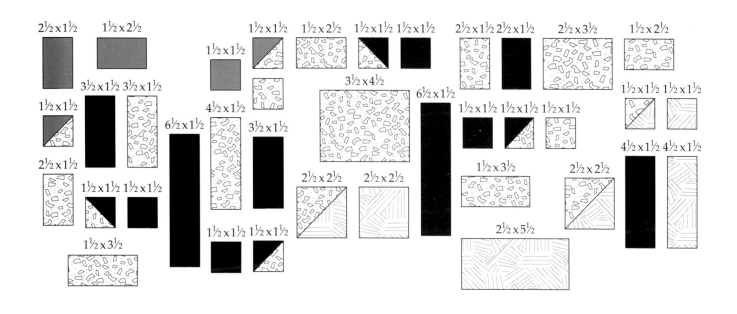

2½ x 1½ 1½ x 2½ 1½ x 1½ 1½ x 2½ 1½ x 1½ 1½ x 1½ 2½ x 1½ 2½ x 1½ 2½ x 3½ 1½ x 2½

1½ x 1½

1½ x 1½ 3½ x 1½ 3½ x 1½ 4½ x 1½ 3½ x 4½ 6½ x 1½ 1½ x 1½ 1½ x 1½ 1½ x 1½ 1½ x 1½ 1½ x 1½

2½ x 1½ 6½ x 1½ 3½ x 1½

1½ x 1½ 1½ x 1½ 2½ x 2½ 2½ x 2½ 1½ x 3½ 2½ x 2½ 4½ x 1½ 4½ x 1½

1½ x 3½ 1½ x 1½ 1½ x 1½ 2½ x 5½

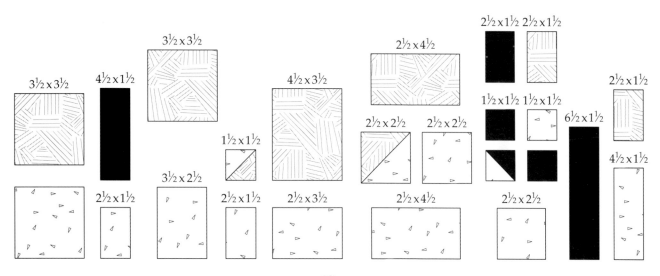

3½ x 3½ 2½ x 4½ 2½ x 1½ 2½ x 1½

3½ x 3½ 4½ x 1½ 4½ x 3½ 1½ x 1½ 1½ x 1½ 2½ x 1½

1½ x 1½ 2½ x 2½ 2½ x 2½ 6½ x 1½

3½ x 2½ 4½ x 1½

2½ x 1½ 2½ x 1½ 2½ x 3½ 2½ x 4½ 2½ x 2½

The Prairies

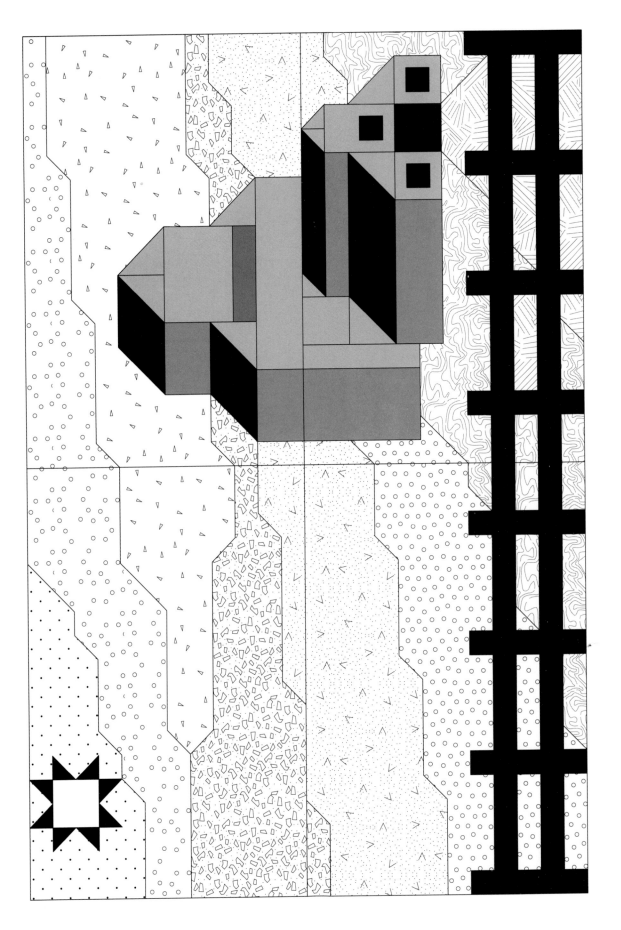

The Prairies

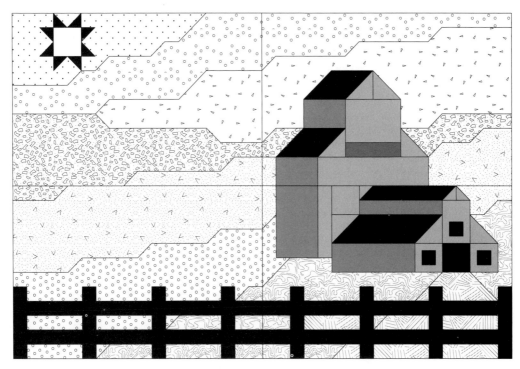

"Heavens Above!" The Prairies

These are the gardens of the Desert, these,
The unshorn fields, boundless and beautiful,
For which the speech of England has no name –
The Prairies. I behold them for the first,
And my heart swells, while the dilated sight
Takes in the encircling vastness. Lo! they stretch...

William Cullen Bryant

No matter how far I travel or what beautiful regions of our land that I visit, my home is on the Prairies and to this I return happily each time. The above excerpt from a poem by William Cullen Bryant aptly describes my feelings about my prairie home.

Before beginning any construction, read Part One of this book for information on fabric selection, color choices and sewing techniques.

In each section of the prairie layout, the graphic at the top of the page shows the section as it would look sewn together. The pieces below are the unfinished sections – with seam allowances.

IMPORTANT NOTE: All traingles and connector corners in the diagrams of the Prairies are constructed from 1½" x 1½" cut squares or 2½" x 2½" cut squares.

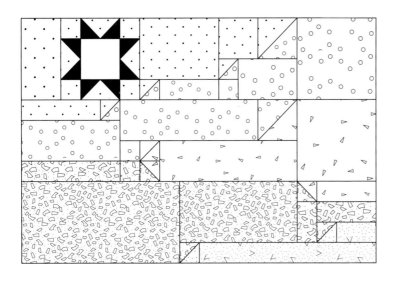

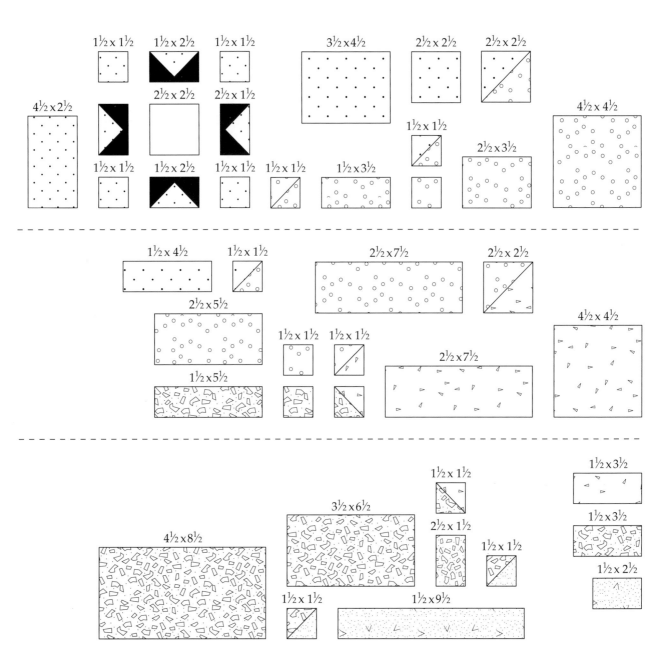

1½ x 1½ 1½ x 2½ 1½ x 1½ 3½ x 4½ 2½ x 2½ 2½ x 2½

4½ x 2½ 2½ x 2½ 2½ x 1½ 4½ x 4½

1½ x 1½ 2½ x 3½

1½ x 1½ 1½ x 2½ 1½ x 1½ 1½ x 1½ 1½ x 3½

1½ x 4½ 1½ x 1½ 2½ x 7½ 2½ x 2½

2½ x 5½ 1½ x 1½ 1½ x 1½ 4½ x 4½

2½ x 7½

1½ x 5½

1½ x 1½ 1½ x 3½

3½ x 6½ 2½ x 1½ 1½ x 3½

4½ x 8½ 1½ x 1½ 1½ x 2½

1½ x 1½ 1½ x 9½

The Prairies
Section Two

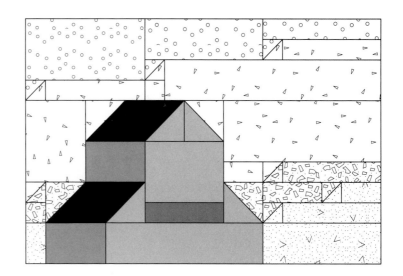

$2\frac{1}{2} \times 6\frac{1}{2}$

$1\frac{1}{2} \times 6\frac{1}{2}$

$3\frac{1}{2} \times 6\frac{1}{2}$

$1\frac{1}{2} \times 1\frac{1}{2}$

$1\frac{1}{2} \times 5\frac{1}{2}$

$1\frac{1}{2} \times 1\frac{1}{2}$

$2\frac{1}{2} \times 11\frac{1}{2}$

$1\frac{1}{2} \times 1\frac{1}{2}$

$1\frac{1}{2} \times 5\frac{1}{2}$

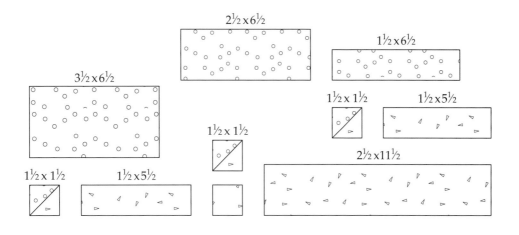

$2\frac{1}{2} \times 2\frac{1}{2}$

$2\frac{1}{2} \times 1\frac{1}{2}$

$2\frac{1}{2} \times 2\frac{1}{2}$

$2\frac{1}{2} \times 2\frac{1}{2}$

$3\frac{1}{2} \times 8\frac{1}{2}$

$4\frac{1}{2} \times 3\frac{1}{2}$

$2\frac{1}{2} \times 3\frac{1}{2}$

$3\frac{1}{2} \times 4\frac{1}{2}$

$1\frac{1}{2} \times 2\frac{1}{2}$

$1\frac{1}{2} \times 1\frac{1}{2}$

$1\frac{1}{2} \times 5\frac{1}{2}$

$1\frac{1}{2} \times 1\frac{1}{2}$

$2\frac{1}{2} \times 2\frac{1}{2}$

$2\frac{1}{2} \times 1\frac{1}{2}$

$2\frac{1}{2} \times 2\frac{1}{2}$

$1\frac{1}{2} \times 3\frac{1}{2}$

$1\frac{1}{2} \times 1\frac{1}{2}$

$1\frac{1}{2} \times 2\frac{1}{2}$

$2\frac{1}{2} \times 2\frac{1}{2}$

$1\frac{1}{2} \times 4\frac{1}{2}$

$1\frac{1}{2} \times 1\frac{1}{2}$

$1\frac{1}{2} \times 5\frac{1}{2}$

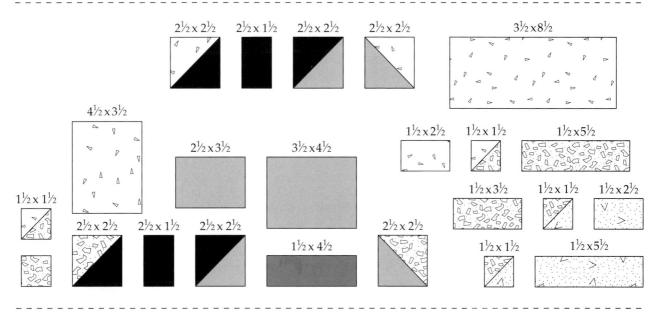

$2\frac{1}{2} \times 1\frac{1}{2}$

$2\frac{1}{2} \times 3\frac{1}{2}$

$2\frac{1}{2} \times 8\frac{1}{2}$

$2\frac{1}{2} \times 6\frac{1}{2}$

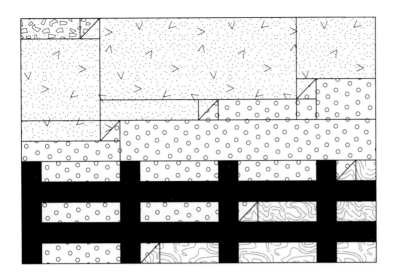

The Prairies
Section Three

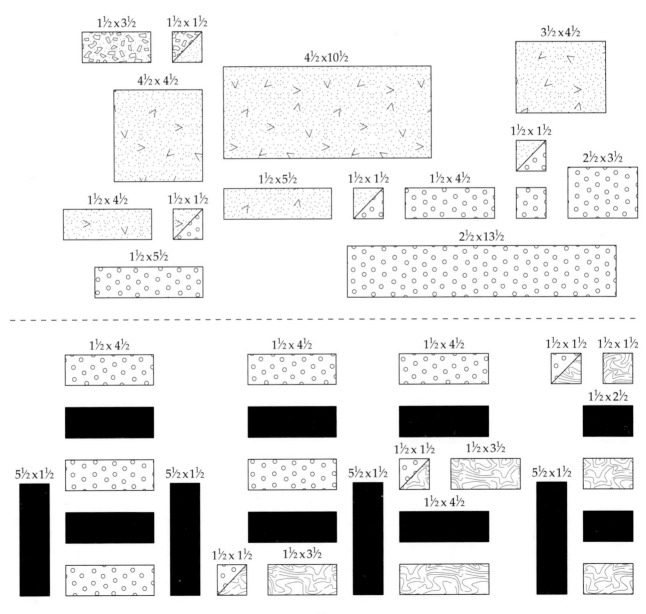

$1\frac{1}{2} \times 3\frac{1}{2}$ $\quad$ $1\frac{1}{2} \times 1\frac{1}{2}$

$3\frac{1}{2} \times 4\frac{1}{2}$

$4\frac{1}{2} \times 4\frac{1}{2}$

$4\frac{1}{2} \times 10\frac{1}{2}$

$1\frac{1}{2} \times 1\frac{1}{2}$

$2\frac{1}{2} \times 3\frac{1}{2}$

$1\frac{1}{2} \times 5\frac{1}{2}$ $\quad$ $1\frac{1}{2} \times 1\frac{1}{2}$ $\quad$ $1\frac{1}{2} \times 4\frac{1}{2}$

$1\frac{1}{2} \times 4\frac{1}{2}$ $\quad$ $1\frac{1}{2} \times 1\frac{1}{2}$

$1\frac{1}{2} \times 5\frac{1}{2}$

$2\frac{1}{2} \times 13\frac{1}{2}$

$1\frac{1}{2} \times 4\frac{1}{2}$ $\qquad$ $1\frac{1}{2} \times 4\frac{1}{2}$ $\qquad$ $1\frac{1}{2} \times 4\frac{1}{2}$ $\qquad$ $1\frac{1}{2} \times 1\frac{1}{2}$ $\quad$ $1\frac{1}{2} \times 1\frac{1}{2}$

$1\frac{1}{2} \times 2\frac{1}{2}$

$1\frac{1}{2} \times 1\frac{1}{2}$ $\quad$ $1\frac{1}{2} \times 3\frac{1}{2}$

$5\frac{1}{2} \times 1\frac{1}{2}$ $\qquad$ $5\frac{1}{2} \times 1\frac{1}{2}$ $\qquad$ $5\frac{1}{2} \times 1\frac{1}{2}$ $\qquad$ $5\frac{1}{2} \times 1\frac{1}{2}$

$1\frac{1}{2} \times 4\frac{1}{2}$

$1\frac{1}{2} \times 1\frac{1}{2}$ $\quad$ $1\frac{1}{2} \times 3\frac{1}{2}$

68

The Prairies
Section Four

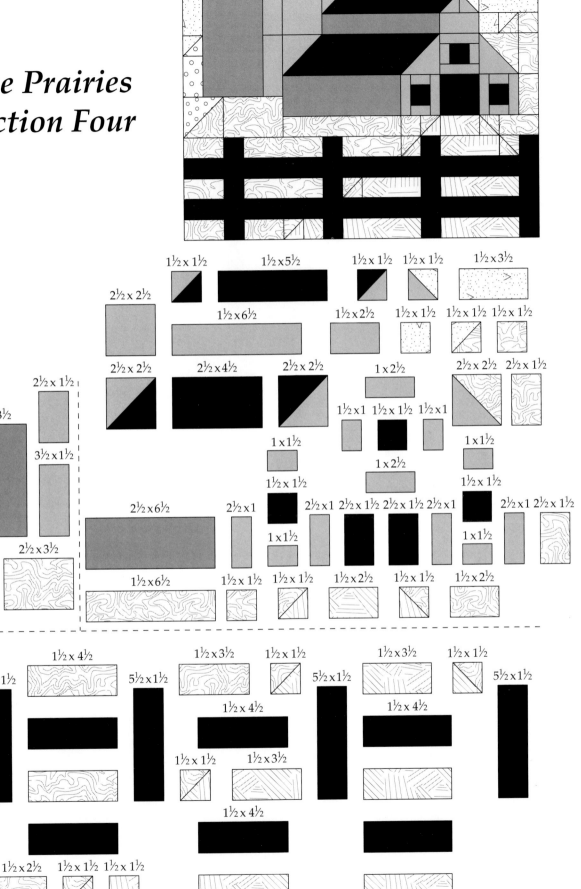

2½ x 1½

1½ x 1½

2½ x 1½

5½ x 3½

2½ x 1½

3½ x 1½

2½ x 2½

2½ x 3½

1½ x 1½

1½ x 5½

1½ x 1½

1½ x 1½

1½ x 3½

2½ x 2½

1½ x 6½

1½ x 2½

1½ x 1½

1½ x 1½ 1½ x 1½

2½ x 2½

2½ x 4½

2½ x 2½

1 x 2½

2½ x 2½ 2½ x 1½

1½ x 1 1½ x 1½ 1½ x 1

1 x 1½

1 x 2½

1 x 1½

1½ x 1½

1½ x 1½

1½ x 1½

2½ x 6½

2½ x 1

2½ x 1 2½ x 1½ 2½ x 1½ 2½ x 1

2½ x 1 2½ x 1½

1 x 1½

1 x 1½

1½ x 6½

1½ x 1½

1½ x 1½

1½ x 2½

1½ x 1½

1½ x 2½

1½ x 2½

5½ x 1½

1½ x 4½

5½ x 1½

1½ x 3½

1½ x 1½

5½ x 1½

1½ x 3½

1½ x 1½

5½ x 1½

1½ x 4½

1½ x 4½

1½ x 1½

1½ x 3½

1½ x 4½

1½ x 2½

1½ x 1½ 1½ x 1½

69

The City

The City

"Heavens Above!" The City

Bustling people, horns honking, bumper to bumper traffic and towering skyscrapers of concrete and glass. Is this what a city is made of? To an extent, yes, as the cities are the core of our civilization. They are the hub of the wheel where much of our economic, political and social existence culminates. But it is not only the buildings and roads that make a city, it is the people. The people design the beautiful city parks and architectural wonders, run the health centers for our care, provide the entertainment – they are the essence of the city. Every city has its own special uniqueness and one only has to look to appreciate the beauty emanated.

Before beginning any construction, read Part One of this book for information on fabric selection, color choices and sewing techniques.

In each section of the city layout, the graphic at the top of the page shows the section as it would look sewn together. The pieces below are the unfinished sections – with seam allowances.

IMPORTANT NOTE: All connector corners or triangles in the city diagrams are constructed from 1½" x 1½" cut squares or 2½" x 2½" cut squares.

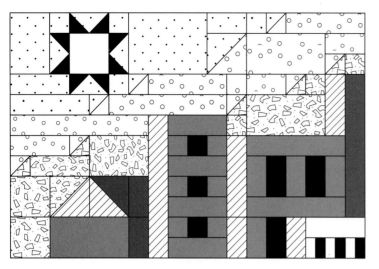

The City
Section One

Part 1	
Part 2	Part 4
Part 3	

Part 1

$1\frac{1}{2}x1\frac{1}{2}$ $1\frac{1}{2}x2\frac{1}{2}$ $1\frac{1}{2}x1\frac{1}{2}$

$3\frac{1}{2}x2\frac{1}{2}$

$1\frac{1}{2}x2\frac{1}{2}$

$1\frac{1}{2}x1\frac{1}{2}$ $1\frac{1}{2}x1\frac{1}{2}$ $1\frac{1}{2}x4\frac{1}{2}$

$2\frac{1}{2}x1\frac{1}{2}$ $2\frac{1}{2}x2\frac{1}{2}$ $2\frac{1}{2}x1\frac{1}{2}$ $3\frac{1}{2}x4\frac{1}{2}$

$2\frac{1}{2}x2\frac{1}{2}$ $2\frac{1}{2}x4\frac{1}{2}$ $1\frac{1}{2}x2\frac{1}{2}$

$1\frac{1}{2}x1\frac{1}{2}$ $1\frac{1}{2}x1\frac{1}{2}$

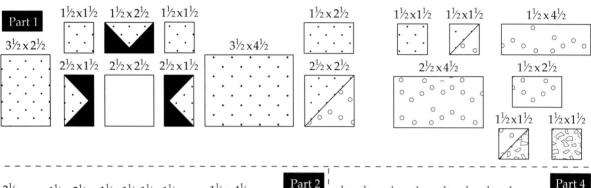

Part 2

$1\frac{1}{2}x3\frac{1}{2}$ $1\frac{1}{2}x2\frac{1}{2}$ $1\frac{1}{2}x1\frac{1}{2}$ $1\frac{1}{2}x1\frac{1}{2}$ $1\frac{1}{2}x4\frac{1}{2}$

$1\frac{1}{2}x4\frac{1}{2}$ $1\frac{1}{2}x1\frac{1}{2}$ $1\frac{1}{2}x6\frac{1}{2}$

Part 4

$1\frac{1}{2}x1\frac{1}{2}$ $1\frac{1}{2}x2\frac{1}{2}$ $1\frac{1}{2}x1\frac{1}{2}$ $1\frac{1}{2}x1\frac{1}{2}$

$3\frac{1}{2}x1\frac{1}{2}$ $7\frac{1}{2}x1\frac{1}{2}$

Part 3

$1\frac{1}{2}x3\frac{1}{2}$

$2\frac{1}{2}x4\frac{1}{2}$

$1\frac{1}{2}x7\frac{1}{2}$

$1\frac{1}{2}x1\frac{1}{2}$ $1\frac{1}{2}x1\frac{1}{2}$ $1\frac{1}{2}x1\frac{1}{2}$

$1\frac{1}{2}x5\frac{1}{2}$

$1\frac{1}{2}x3\frac{1}{2}$ $1\frac{1}{2}x1\frac{1}{2}$

$1\frac{1}{2}x3\frac{1}{2}$

$4\frac{1}{2}x1\frac{1}{2}$ $2\frac{1}{2}x1\frac{1}{2}$ $2\frac{1}{2}x1\frac{1}{2}$ $2\frac{1}{2}x1\frac{1}{2}$ $2\frac{1}{2}x1\frac{1}{2}$ $2\frac{1}{2}x1\frac{1}{2}$

$1\frac{1}{2}x1\frac{1}{2}$ $1\frac{1}{2}x3\frac{1}{2}$

$7\frac{1}{2}x1\frac{1}{2}$

$1\frac{1}{2}x1\frac{1}{2}$ $1\frac{1}{2}x1\frac{1}{2}$ $1\frac{1}{2}x1\frac{1}{2}$

$1\frac{1}{2}x3\frac{1}{2}$

$1\frac{1}{2}x5\frac{1}{2}$

$2\frac{1}{2}x2\frac{1}{2}$ $2\frac{1}{2}x2\frac{1}{2}$ $2\frac{1}{2}x2\frac{1}{2}$ $2\frac{1}{2}x1\frac{1}{2}$

$1\frac{1}{2}x1\frac{1}{2}$ $1\frac{1}{2}x1\frac{1}{2}$ $1\frac{1}{2}x1\frac{1}{2}$

$2\frac{1}{2}x1\frac{1}{2}$ $2\frac{1}{2}x1\frac{1}{2}$ $2\frac{1}{2}x1\frac{1}{2}$ $2\frac{1}{2}x1\frac{1}{2}$

$2\frac{1}{2}x4\frac{1}{2}$ $2\frac{1}{2}x1\frac{1}{2}$

$1\frac{1}{2}x3\frac{1}{2}$

$1\frac{1}{2}x3\frac{1}{2}$

$1\frac{1}{2}x1$ $1\frac{1}{2}x1$ $1\frac{1}{2}x1$ $1\frac{1}{2}x1$ $1\frac{1}{2}x1$ $1\frac{1}{2}x1$

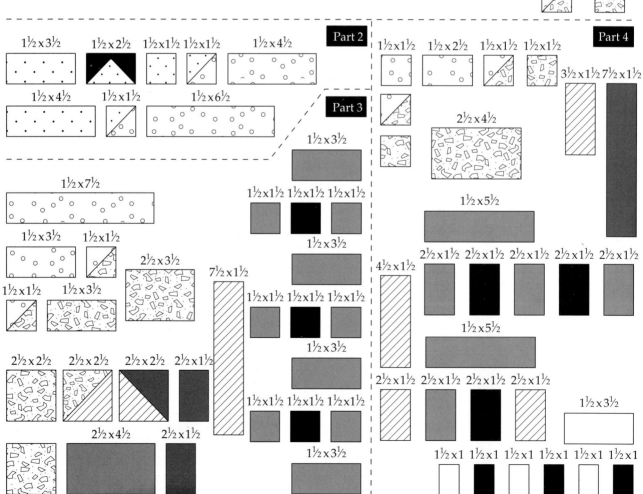

The City
Section Two

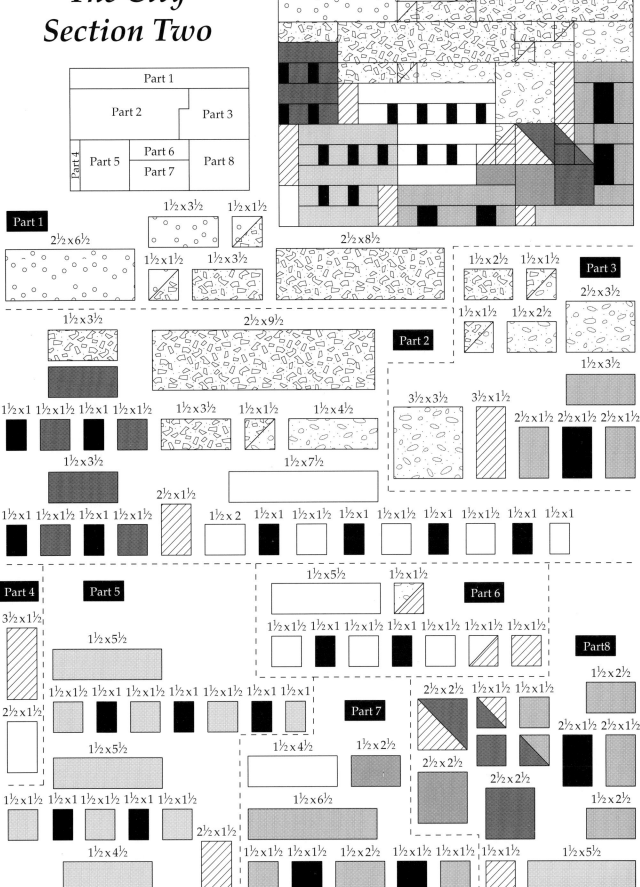

Part 1

$2\frac{1}{2} \times 6\frac{1}{2}$

$1\frac{1}{2} \times 3\frac{1}{2}$

$1\frac{1}{2} \times 1\frac{1}{2}$

$1\frac{1}{2} \times 1\frac{1}{2}$

$1\frac{1}{2} \times 3\frac{1}{2}$

$2\frac{1}{2} \times 8\frac{1}{2}$

$1\frac{1}{2} \times 2\frac{1}{2}$

$1\frac{1}{2} \times 1\frac{1}{2}$

Part 3

$2\frac{1}{2} \times 3\frac{1}{2}$

$1\frac{1}{2} \times 1\frac{1}{2}$

$1\frac{1}{2} \times 2\frac{1}{2}$

$1\frac{1}{2} \times 3\frac{1}{2}$

$1\frac{1}{2} \times 3\frac{1}{2}$

$2\frac{1}{2} \times 9\frac{1}{2}$

Part 2

$1\frac{1}{2} \times 1$

$1\frac{1}{2} \times 1\frac{1}{2}$

$1\frac{1}{2} \times 1$

$1\frac{1}{2} \times 1\frac{1}{2}$

$1\frac{1}{2} \times 3\frac{1}{2}$

$1\frac{1}{2} \times 1\frac{1}{2}$

$1\frac{1}{2} \times 4\frac{1}{2}$

$3\frac{1}{2} \times 3\frac{1}{2}$

$3\frac{1}{2} \times 1\frac{1}{2}$

$2\frac{1}{2} \times 1\frac{1}{2}$

$2\frac{1}{2} \times 1\frac{1}{2}$

$2\frac{1}{2} \times 1\frac{1}{2}$

$1\frac{1}{2} \times 3\frac{1}{2}$

$1\frac{1}{2} \times 7\frac{1}{2}$

$1\frac{1}{2} \times 1$

$1\frac{1}{2} \times 1\frac{1}{2}$

$1\frac{1}{2} \times 1$

$1\frac{1}{2} \times 1\frac{1}{2}$

$2\frac{1}{2} \times 1\frac{1}{2}$

$1\frac{1}{2} \times 2$

$1\frac{1}{2} \times 1$

$1\frac{1}{2} \times 1\frac{1}{2}$

$1\frac{1}{2} \times 1$

$1\frac{1}{2} \times 1\frac{1}{2}$

$1\frac{1}{2} \times 1$

$1\frac{1}{2} \times 1\frac{1}{2}$

$1\frac{1}{2} \times 1$

$1\frac{1}{2} \times 1$

Part 4

Part 5

Part 6

$1\frac{1}{2} \times 5\frac{1}{2}$

$1\frac{1}{2} \times 1\frac{1}{2}$

$3\frac{1}{2} \times 1\frac{1}{2}$

$1\frac{1}{2} \times 1\frac{1}{2}$

$1\frac{1}{2} \times 1$

$1\frac{1}{2} \times 1\frac{1}{2}$

$1\frac{1}{2} \times 1$

$1\frac{1}{2} \times 1\frac{1}{2}$

$1\frac{1}{2} \times 1\frac{1}{2}$

$1\frac{1}{2} \times 1\frac{1}{2}$

$1\frac{1}{2} \times 1\frac{1}{2}$

Part8

$1\frac{1}{2} \times 5\frac{1}{2}$

$2\frac{1}{2} \times 2\frac{1}{2}$

$1\frac{1}{2} \times 1\frac{1}{2}$

$1\frac{1}{2} \times 1\frac{1}{2}$

$1\frac{1}{2} \times 2\frac{1}{2}$

$2\frac{1}{2} \times 1\frac{1}{2}$

$1\frac{1}{2} \times 1\frac{1}{2}$

$1\frac{1}{2} \times 1$

$1\frac{1}{2} \times 1\frac{1}{2}$

$1\frac{1}{2} \times 1$

$1\frac{1}{2} \times 1\frac{1}{2}$

$1\frac{1}{2} \times 1$

$1\frac{1}{2} \times 1$

Part 7

$2\frac{1}{2} \times 2\frac{1}{2}$

$2\frac{1}{2} \times 1\frac{1}{2}$

$2\frac{1}{2} \times 1\frac{1}{2}$

$1\frac{1}{2} \times 4\frac{1}{2}$

$1\frac{1}{2} \times 2\frac{1}{2}$

$2\frac{1}{2} \times 2\frac{1}{2}$

$1\frac{1}{2} \times 2\frac{1}{2}$

$1\frac{1}{2} \times 5\frac{1}{2}$

$2\frac{1}{2} \times 1\frac{1}{2}$

$1\frac{1}{2} \times 1\frac{1}{2}$

$1\frac{1}{2} \times 1$

$1\frac{1}{2} \times 1\frac{1}{2}$

$1\frac{1}{2} \times 1$

$1\frac{1}{2} \times 1\frac{1}{2}$

$1\frac{1}{2} \times 4\frac{1}{2}$

$2\frac{1}{2} \times 1\frac{1}{2}$

$1\frac{1}{2} \times 6\frac{1}{2}$

$1\frac{1}{2} \times 1\frac{1}{2}$

$1\frac{1}{2} \times 1\frac{1}{2}$

$1\frac{1}{2} \times 2\frac{1}{2}$

$1\frac{1}{2} \times 1\frac{1}{2}$

$1\frac{1}{2} \times 1\frac{1}{2}$

$1\frac{1}{2} \times 1\frac{1}{2}$

$1\frac{1}{2} \times 5\frac{1}{2}$

The City
Section Three

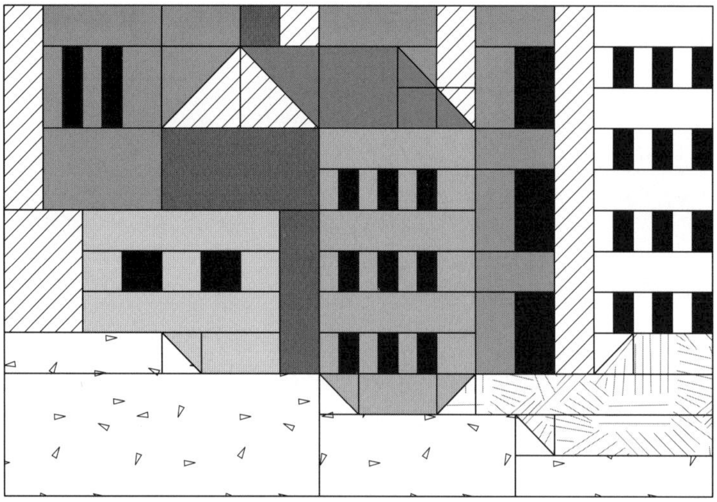

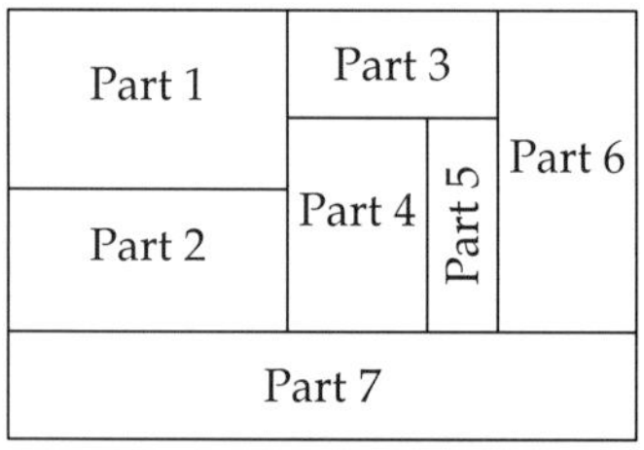

Part 1
Part 2
Part 3
Part 4
Part 5
Part 6
Part 7

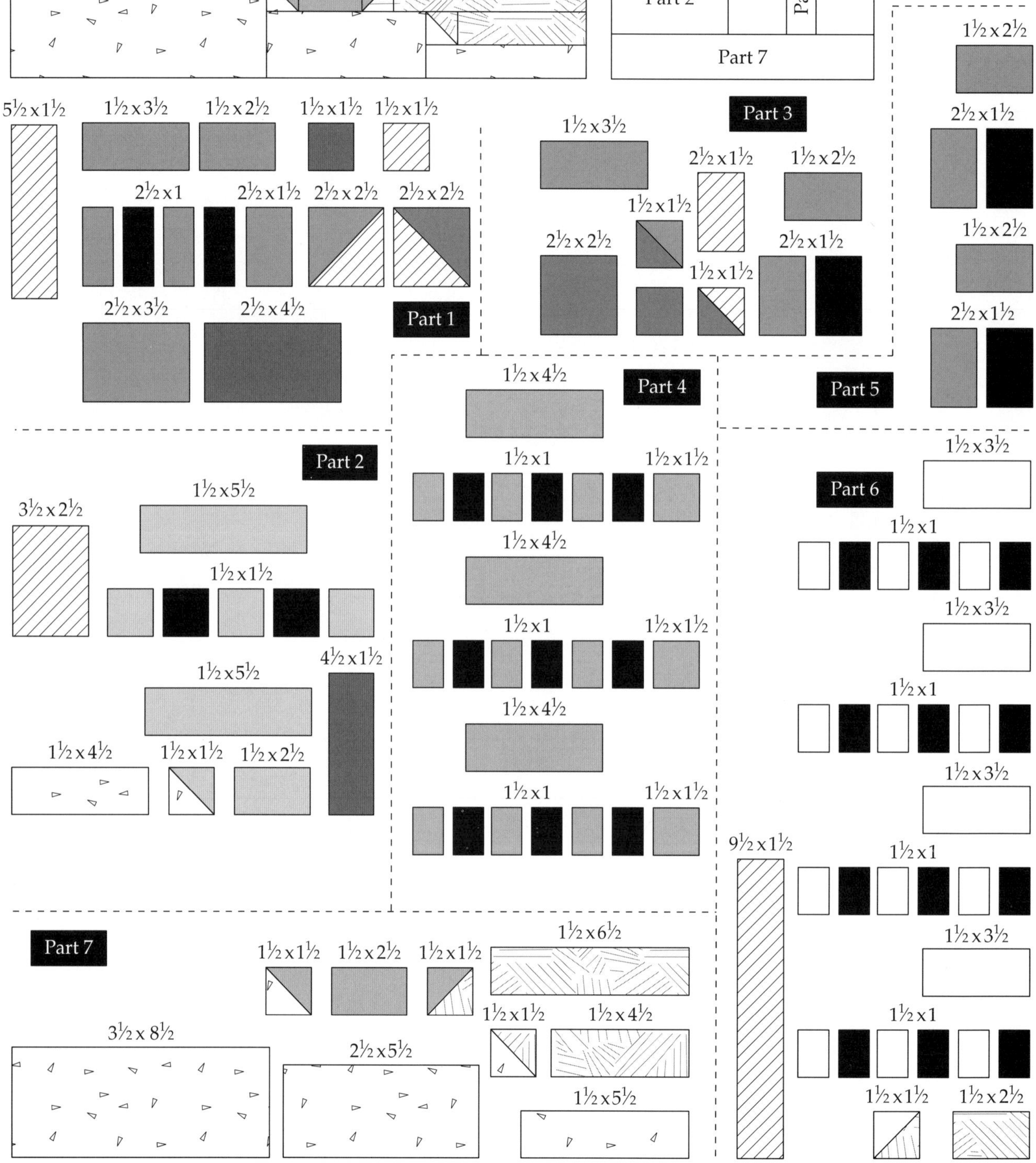

Part 1
5½ x 1½
1½ x 3½
1½ x 2½
1½ x 1½
1½ x 1½
2½ x 1
2½ x 1½
2½ x 2½
2½ x 2½
2½ x 3½
2½ x 4½
Part 3
1½ x 3½
2½ x 1½
1½ x 2½
1½ x 1½
2½ x 2½
1½ x 1½
2½ x 1½
Part 5
1½ x 2½
2½ x 1½
1½ x 2½
2½ x 1½
Part 2
3½ x 2½
1½ x 5½
1½ x 1½
1½ x 5½
4½ x 1½
1½ x 4½
1½ x 1½
1½ x 2½
Part 4
1½ x 4½
1½ x 1
1½ x 1½
1½ x 4½
1½ x 1
1½ x 1½
1½ x 4½
1½ x 1
1½ x 1½
Part 6
1½ x 3½
1½ x 1
1½ x 3½
1½ x 1
1½ x 3½
9½ x 1½
1½ x 1
1½ x 3½
1½ x 1
1½ x 1½
1½ x 2½
Part 7
1½ x 1½
1½ x 2½
1½ x 1½
1½ x 6½
1½ x 1½
1½ x 4½
3½ x 8½
2½ x 5½
1½ x 5½

The City
Section Four

$1\frac{1}{2} \times 1\frac{1}{2}$ $1\frac{1}{2} \times 1$ $1\frac{1}{2} \times 1\frac{1}{2}$ $1\frac{1}{2} \times 1$ $1\frac{1}{2} \times 1\frac{1}{2}$

$1\frac{1}{2} \times 4\frac{1}{2}$

$1\frac{1}{2} \times 1\frac{1}{2}$ $1\frac{1}{2} \times 1$ $1\frac{1}{2} \times 1\frac{1}{2}$ $1\frac{1}{2} \times 1$ $1\frac{1}{2} \times 1\frac{1}{2}$

$1\frac{1}{2} \times 4\frac{1}{2}$

$1\frac{1}{2} \times 1\frac{1}{2}$ $1\frac{1}{2} \times 1$ $1\frac{1}{2} \times 1\frac{1}{2}$ $1\frac{1}{2} \times 1$ $1\frac{1}{2} \times 1\frac{1}{2}$

$1\frac{1}{2} \times 4\frac{1}{2}$

$1\frac{1}{2} \times 1\frac{1}{2}$ $1\frac{1}{2} \times 1$ $1\frac{1}{2} \times 1\frac{1}{2}$ $1\frac{1}{2} \times 1$ $1\frac{1}{2} \times 1\frac{1}{2}$

$7\frac{1}{2} \times 1\frac{1}{2}$

$1\frac{1}{2} \times 6\frac{1}{2}$

$1\frac{1}{2} \times 1\frac{1}{2}$ $1\frac{1}{2} \times 2\frac{1}{2}$ $1\frac{1}{2} \times 1\frac{1}{2}$

$5\frac{1}{2} \times 1\frac{1}{2}$

$1\frac{1}{2} \times 6\frac{1}{2}$

$1\frac{1}{2} \times 1\frac{1}{2}$ $1\frac{1}{2} \times 2\frac{1}{2}$ $1\frac{1}{2} \times 1\frac{1}{2}$

$1\frac{1}{2} \times 6\frac{1}{2}$

$1\frac{1}{2} \times 1\frac{1}{2}$ $1\frac{1}{2} \times 2\frac{1}{2}$ $1\frac{1}{2} \times 1\frac{1}{2}$

$1\frac{1}{2} \times 5\frac{1}{2}$

$7\frac{1}{2} \times 1\frac{1}{2}$

$2\frac{1}{2} \times 1\frac{1}{2}$

$1\frac{1}{2} \times 5\frac{1}{2}$

$1\frac{1}{2} \times 3\frac{1}{2}$

$2\frac{1}{2} \times 1\frac{1}{2}$

$1\frac{1}{2} \times 1\frac{1}{2}$

$2\frac{1}{2} \times 5\frac{1}{2}$

$1\frac{1}{2} \times 1\frac{1}{2}$ $1\frac{1}{2} \times 15\frac{1}{2}$

$2\frac{1}{2} \times 8\frac{1}{2}$ $1\frac{1}{2} \times 6\frac{1}{2}$ $1\frac{1}{2} \times 1\frac{1}{2}$ $1\frac{1}{2} \times 3\frac{1}{2}$

$1\frac{1}{2} \times 1\frac{1}{2}$

$1\frac{1}{2} \times 1\frac{1}{2}$

$2\frac{1}{2} \times 7\frac{1}{2}$ $2\frac{1}{2} \times 1\frac{1}{2}$ $3\frac{1}{2} \times 9\frac{1}{2}$

75

Accessories

Pillow

Fabric Requirements:

⅝ yard – main fabric for ruffle
⅛ yard – for accent border
⅓ yard – for pillow back

Small pieces of fabric for piecework. These may coordinate with the quilt or be unique to the pillow.

Directions. Piece the pillow front following the chart. The piecework should measure 15½" x 15½" raw edge to raw edge.

Cut two strips of accent border 1½" wide. Sew these to the piecework log cabin style, i.e., two sides, then the top, then the bottom.

Ruffle. Cut three strips 6½" wide. Stitch these together end to end to form a circle of ruffle. Press in half lengthwise, wrong sides together. Zig-zag over a gather cord close to the raw edges. Mark the ruffle into four equal sections. Mark the centers of the four sides of the pillow top. Lay the ruffle right sides together on the pillow top, matching quarter markings. Gather the ruffle to fit the pillow and pin. See Figure 22.

Pillow Back. Cut one strip 10" wide. From this strip sub-cut two pieces 10" x 16½". Fold under ¼" hemstitch on one 16½" side of each piece. Lay the two backs right sides together and raw edges even on the pillow top and ruffle. The two backs will overlap in the middle to form the opening for the pillow form. Stitch around the four sides of the pillow being careful that the ruffle does not get folded out of position. Turn to the right side and insert the pillow form.

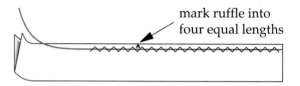

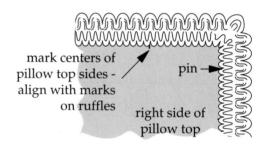

Figure 22. Making a ruffle.

Placemats

Fabric Requirements:

⅓ yard – for outside border
⅙ yard – for accent border
½ yard – for binding
1 yard – for backing
1 yard – 45" thermolam

Small pieces of fabric for piecework. These may coordinate with the quilt or be unique to the placemats.

Directions. Piece the placemat front following the chart. The piecework should measure 8½" x 14½" from raw edge to raw edge.

Cut two strips of accent fabric 1" wide. Stitch these to the piecework log cabin style. (Sides and then top and bottom.) Cut two strips of main fabric 2" wide. Stitch these to the piecework in the same manner as the accent border. The placemat top should now be 12½" x 18½".

Cut a piece of thermolam and a piece of backing 12½" x 18½". Layer the backing, thermolam and placemat top. Pin well. You may or may not wish to do some quilting on the placemat at this point. I find some quilting holds the placemat together better for future washing and also enhances the design.

Make the straight strip binding following the steps given in the General Instructions section, Binding Method #1. You will need approximately 62" of binding for each placemat. Apply the binding to the placemat using Binding Method #1.

Apron

Fabric Requirements:

   1⅛ yard – main fabric
   ⅛ yard – for accent border
   ¾ yard – for bib and band lining

Small pieces of fabric for piecing the bib and band. These may be the same fabric used in the quilt or unique to the apron.

Bib. Construct the bib following the diagram. The piecework borders should measure 8½" x 8½". Cut a strip of accent border 1" wide. Stitch the border to the bib piecework log cabin style (two sides, then the top). Press. Cut a strip of main border 2" wide. Stitch using the same method. The bib should measure 12½" x 12½".

Ties. Cut three strips of main fabric 5" wide by the width of the fabric. Cut one of these strips in half. Stitch one short strip to each of the two long strips. Fold in half lengthwise, right sides together and stitch the long side ONLY. Refold one end of the tie so that the seam is in the middle and stitch across the end. Turn right sides out and press. See Figure 23.

sew short strip to long strip; fold lengthwise
right sides together and stitch length

refold lengthwise with seam
centered and stitch across the end

Figure 23. Making the apron ties.

Bib and Tie Construction. Cut a 12½" x 12½" piece of thermolam. Lay the pieced bib square right side up on the thermolam. NOTE - you may wish to do some quilting on the bib and thermolam. Lay the raw ends of the bib ties right sides together on the pieced bib, ¼" in from the edge. See Figure 24.

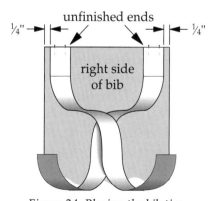

unfinished ends
¼"   ¼"
right side
of bib

Figure 24. Placing the bib ties.

Pin the ties to the piecework and thermolam. Fold the ties towards the center and pin so they do not get caught in the stitching. Lay the lining piece right sides together on the piecework, thermolam and ties, and pin. Stitch on three sides leaving the bottom open. Clip corners, turn and press.

The **Bottom Band**. Construct the bottom band following the two diagrams. Join the left and right sections together to form the bottom band. The piecework should measure 8½" x 40½". Cut a strip of accent border 1½" wide. Stitch the accent strip to the top long edge of the band. Cut a strip of lining fabric – 9½" wide x 40½" long. Lay the band and the lining right sides together and stitch on three sides, leaving the top open. Turn right side out and press.

The **Apron Skirt**. Cut a piece of main fabric 18" x 41". Fold under and press ¼" and ¼" on each short side and hemstitch. See Figure 25.

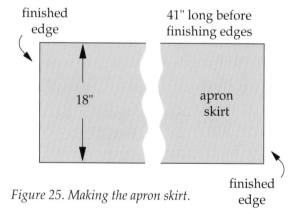

Figure 25. Making the apron skirt.

Apron Construction. Skirt and Band– stitch the right side of the apron skirt to the top right side of the pieced band and stitch being careful to leave the lining of the band free. Fold under ¼" on the lining and hand stitch or machine stitch in place.

Waistband and Bib – cut two pieces 2½" x 18½" from the main fabric. Cut two pieces 7" x 2" for the waistband loops and sew into loops by folding each long side to the center twice and stitch ⅛" from the folded edge. Place the waistband right side up, center the bib right side up on that piece, pin loops to the waistband ends. See Figure 26.

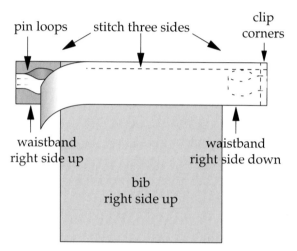

Figure 26. Placing the waistband on the bib.

Place the second waistband right sides down on the bib and the first waistband. Stitch three sides, leaving the bottom open, clip corners and turn. Gather the apron skirt to fit the waistband, stitch the lining of the waistband to the wrong side of the skirt. Fold under ¼" on the waistband and press. Topstitch the waistband onto the apron skirt.

Potholder

Fabric Requirements:

10" x 10" – for backing
10" x 10" – thermolam
¾ yard – for bib and band lining

Small pieces of fabric for piecing that may match the quilt or be unique to the potholder.

78

Directions. Piece the potholder front following the chart. The piecework should measure 8½" x 8½"raw edge to raw edge.

Cut a 1½" x 4½" piece of fabric for the tab. Fold under ¼" on each long side to the wrong side and press. Fold in half and top stitch along the folded edge. Position the tab in the center of the top edge of the potholder and stitch to hold. See Figure 27.

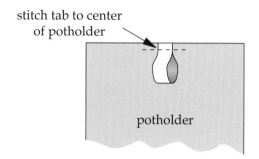

Figure 27. Placing the hook on the potholder.

Lay the front piecework right sides together on the 10" square of the backing fabric. Lay the 10" square of the thermolam under the backing. The piecework will be smaller than the rest, so just center it on the backing. Stitch around with a ¼" seam, leaving 2" open on the bottom edge. Turn to the right side and hand stitch the opening.

You may wish to do some quilting on the piecework at this time.

Tablerunner

Table Runner #1. This variation consists of sky background and a sprinkling of stars and measures 14" x 18". There are four sections in this table runner.

Table Runner #2. This one measures 16" x 64" including borders. This variation consists of a sky and a scene and was designed to coordinate with the *Heavens Above the Desert* quilt. If you wish to make this runner to coordinate with one of the other quilts, try replacing the lower two sections with a portion of the scene from the quilt of your choice. There may be adjustments required, but don't be intimidated.

Fabric Requirements:

Tablerunner #1:

⅛ yard – for inside border
¾ yard – for bib and band lining
¼ yard of main fabric for the outside border
⅞ yard of fabric for backing
⅓ yard of fabric for the binding
14" x 48" piece of thermolam

Small pieces of fabric for the piecework. You will probably need ⅛ yard cuts of fabric for each of the backgrounds.

Tablerunner #2:

⅛ yard of accent for the inside border
¼ yard of main fabric for the outside border
1 yard of fabric for the backing
⅓ yard of fabric for the binding
⅓ yard of fabric for the binding
16" x 64" piece of thermolam

Small pieces of fabric for piecing. You will probably need ⅛ yard cuts of fabric for each of the backgrounds.

Directions. Piece the table runner front following the chart. The piecework should measure: Tablerunner #1: 10½" x 44½"; Table runner #2: 12½" x 60½".

Cut the following strips for borders: Tablerunner #1: Accent – three strips 1" wide; Outside Border – four strips 2" wide; Tablerunner #2: Accent – four strips 1" wide; Outside Border – four strips 2" wide. Stitch these border pieces to the piecework log cabin style. (Refer to Border Applications in the General Instructions.

Cut a piece of thermolam the size required. If you do not have a piece large enough, you may have to piece together two sections. Refer to Layering in the General Instructions.

Layer the backing, thermolam and table runner top. Pin well with safety pins. You may or may not wish to do some quilting at this point. I find that some quilting holds the table runner together better for future washing and also enhances the design.

Make the straight strip binding following the steps given in the General Instructions, Binding Method #1.

Potholder

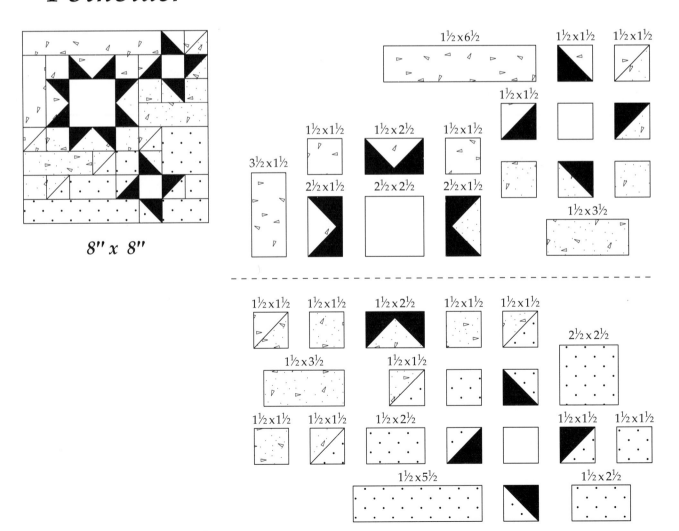

8" x 8"

Pillow

16" x 16"

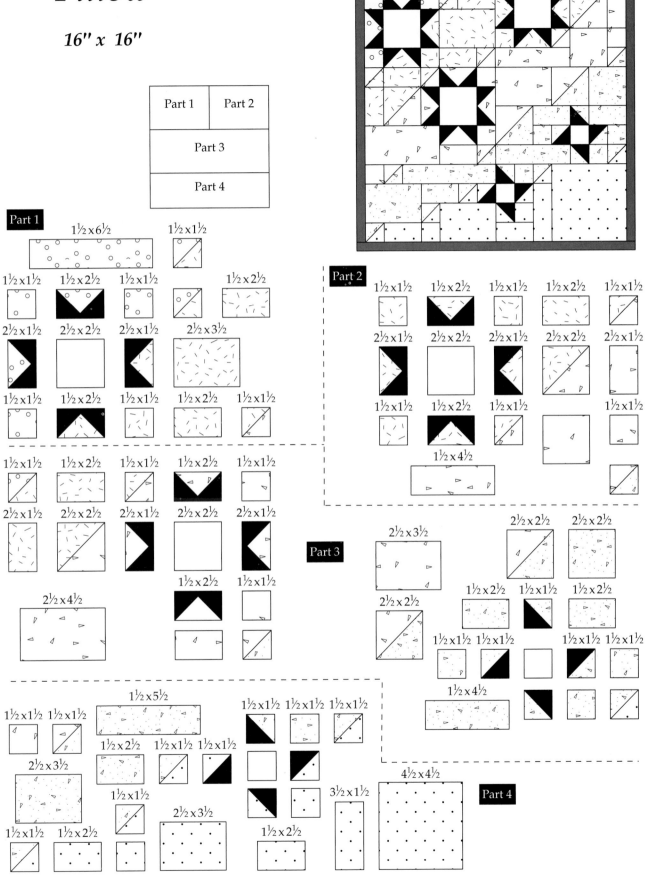

Part 1	Part 2
Part 3	
Part 4	

Part 1

$1\frac{1}{2} \times 6\frac{1}{2}$ $1\frac{1}{2} \times 1\frac{1}{2}$

$1\frac{1}{2} \times 1\frac{1}{2}$ $1\frac{1}{2} \times 2\frac{1}{2}$ $1\frac{1}{2} \times 1\frac{1}{2}$ $1\frac{1}{2} \times 2\frac{1}{2}$

$2\frac{1}{2} \times 1\frac{1}{2}$ $2\frac{1}{2} \times 2\frac{1}{2}$ $2\frac{1}{2} \times 1\frac{1}{2}$ $2\frac{1}{2} \times 3\frac{1}{2}$

$1\frac{1}{2} \times 1\frac{1}{2}$ $1\frac{1}{2} \times 2\frac{1}{2}$ $1\frac{1}{2} \times 1\frac{1}{2}$ $1\frac{1}{2} \times 2\frac{1}{2}$ $1\frac{1}{2} \times 1\frac{1}{2}$

$1\frac{1}{2} \times 1\frac{1}{2}$ $1\frac{1}{2} \times 2\frac{1}{2}$ $1\frac{1}{2} \times 1\frac{1}{2}$ $1\frac{1}{2} \times 2\frac{1}{2}$ $1\frac{1}{2} \times 1\frac{1}{2}$

$2\frac{1}{2} \times 1\frac{1}{2}$ $2\frac{1}{2} \times 2\frac{1}{2}$ $2\frac{1}{2} \times 1\frac{1}{2}$ $2\frac{1}{2} \times 2\frac{1}{2}$ $2\frac{1}{2} \times 1\frac{1}{2}$

$1\frac{1}{2} \times 2\frac{1}{2}$ $1\frac{1}{2} \times 1\frac{1}{2}$

$2\frac{1}{2} \times 4\frac{1}{2}$

Part 2

$1\frac{1}{2} \times 1\frac{1}{2}$ $1\frac{1}{2} \times 2\frac{1}{2}$ $1\frac{1}{2} \times 1\frac{1}{2}$ $1\frac{1}{2} \times 2\frac{1}{2}$ $1\frac{1}{2} \times 1\frac{1}{2}$

$2\frac{1}{2} \times 1\frac{1}{2}$ $2\frac{1}{2} \times 2\frac{1}{2}$ $2\frac{1}{2} \times 1\frac{1}{2}$ $2\frac{1}{2} \times 2\frac{1}{2}$ $2\frac{1}{2} \times 1\frac{1}{2}$

$1\frac{1}{2} \times 1\frac{1}{2}$ $1\frac{1}{2} \times 2\frac{1}{2}$ $1\frac{1}{2} \times 1\frac{1}{2}$ $1\frac{1}{2} \times 1\frac{1}{2}$

$1\frac{1}{2} \times 4\frac{1}{2}$

Part 3

$2\frac{1}{2} \times 3\frac{1}{2}$ $2\frac{1}{2} \times 2\frac{1}{2}$ $2\frac{1}{2} \times 2\frac{1}{2}$

$2\frac{1}{2} \times 2\frac{1}{2}$ $1\frac{1}{2} \times 2\frac{1}{2}$ $1\frac{1}{2} \times 1\frac{1}{2}$ $1\frac{1}{2} \times 2\frac{1}{2}$

$1\frac{1}{2} \times 1\frac{1}{2}$ $1\frac{1}{2} \times 1\frac{1}{2}$ $1\frac{1}{2} \times 1\frac{1}{2}$ $1\frac{1}{2} \times 1\frac{1}{2}$

$1\frac{1}{2} \times 4\frac{1}{2}$

Part 4

$1\frac{1}{2} \times 5\frac{1}{2}$

$1\frac{1}{2} \times 1\frac{1}{2}$ $1\frac{1}{2} \times 1\frac{1}{2}$ $1\frac{1}{2} \times 1\frac{1}{2}$ $1\frac{1}{2} \times 1\frac{1}{2}$ $1\frac{1}{2} \times 1\frac{1}{2}$

$1\frac{1}{2} \times 2\frac{1}{2}$ $1\frac{1}{2} \times 1\frac{1}{2}$ $1\frac{1}{2} \times 1\frac{1}{2}$

$2\frac{1}{2} \times 3\frac{1}{2}$ $1\frac{1}{2} \times 1\frac{1}{2}$

$3\frac{1}{2} \times 1\frac{1}{2}$ $4\frac{1}{2} \times 4\frac{1}{2}$

$1\frac{1}{2} \times 1\frac{1}{2}$ $1\frac{1}{2} \times 2\frac{1}{2}$ $2\frac{1}{2} \times 3\frac{1}{2}$ $1\frac{1}{2} \times 2\frac{1}{2}$

81

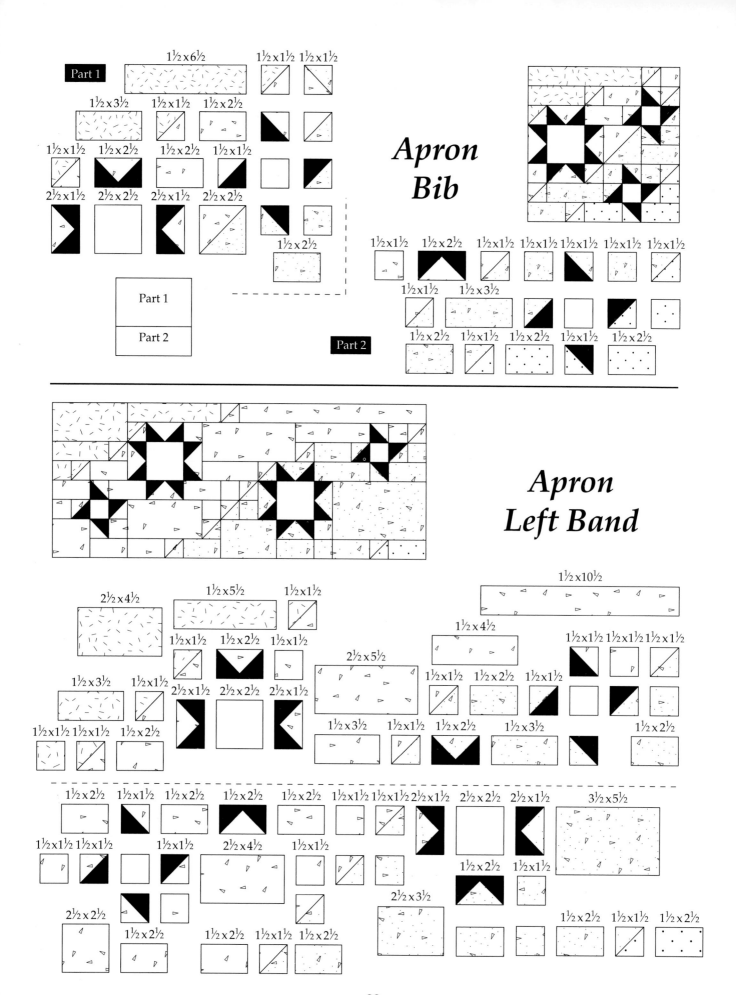

Apron
Right Band

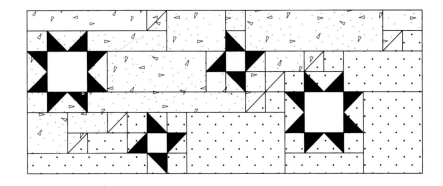

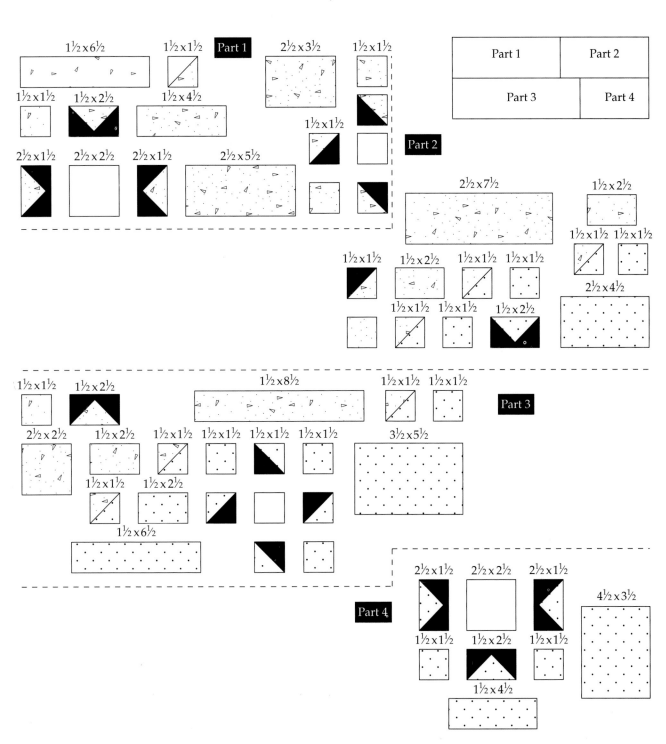

1½ x 6½   1½ x 1½   **Part 1**   2½ x 3½   1½ x 1½

1½ x 1½   1½ x 2½   1½ x 4½

1½ x 1½

2½ x 1½   2½ x 2½   2½ x 1½   2½ x 5½

| Part 1 | Part 2 |
| Part 3 | Part 4 |

Part 2

2½ x 7½   1½ x 2½

1½ x 1½   1½ x 1½

1½ x 1½   1½ x 2½   1½ x 1½   1½ x 1½

2½ x 4½

1½ x 1½   1½ x 1½   1½ x 2½

1½ x 1½   1½ x 2½   1½ x 8½   1½ x 1½   1½ x 1½   **Part 3**

2½ x 2½   1½ x 2½   1½ x 1½   1½ x 1½   1½ x 1½   1½ x 1½   3½ x 5½

1½ x 1½   1½ x 2½

1½ x 6½

Part 4   2½ x 1½   2½ x 2½   2½ x 1½   4½ x 3½

1½ x 1½   1½ x 2½   1½ x 1½

1½ x 4½

83

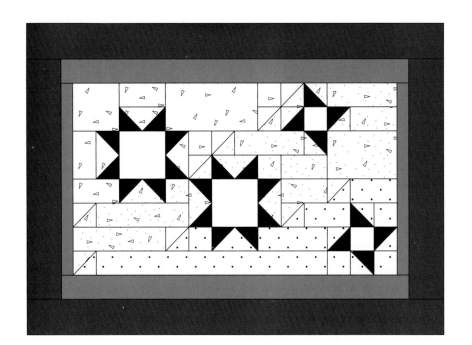

Placemat

12" x 18"

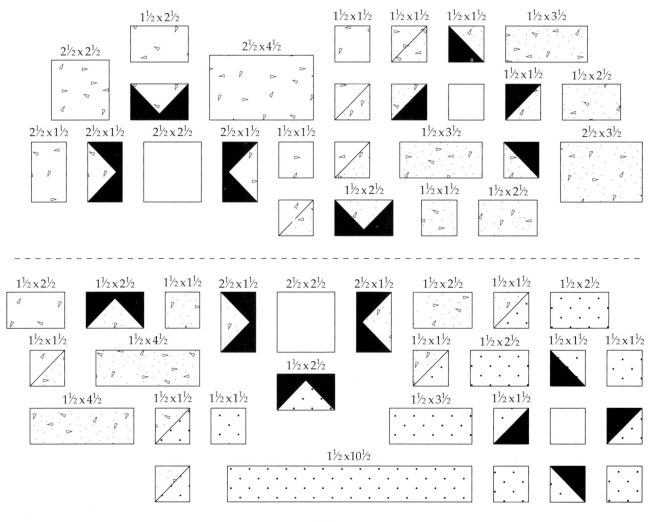

Tablerunners

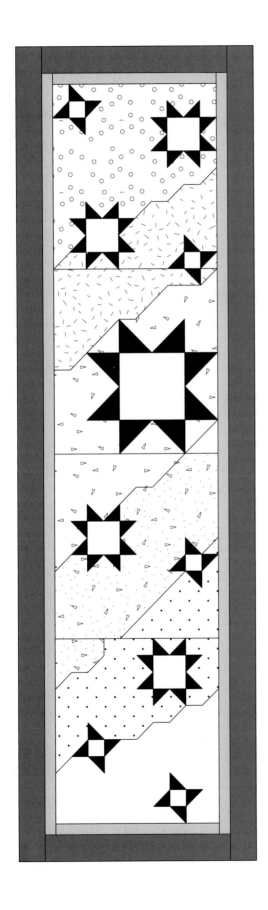

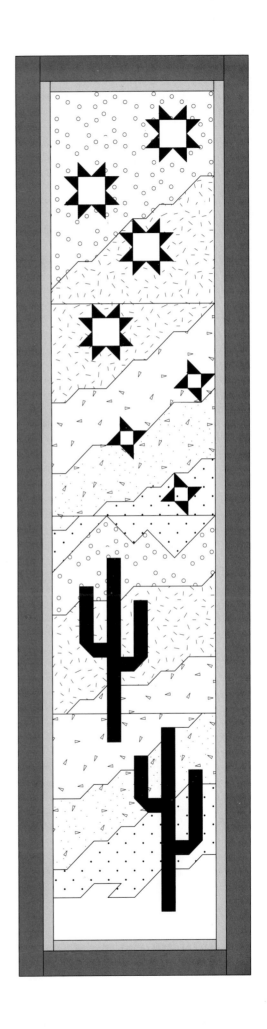

Tablerunner #1

14" x 48"

1½x1½ 1½x1½ 1½x1½ 2½ x 4½ 1½ x 2½ 2½ x 1½

2½ x 2½ 3½ x 4½ 2½ x 1½ 2½ x 2½ 2½ x 1½

1½x1½ 1½ x 2½ 1½x1½

2½ x 7½ 1½x1½ 1½ x 2½

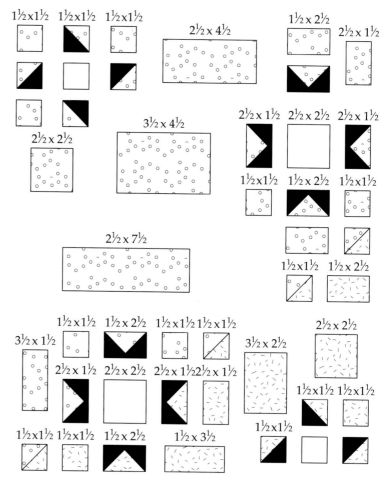

Section 1

3½ x 1½ 1½x1½ 1½ x 2½ 1½x1½ 1½x1½ 3½ x 2½ 2½ x 2½

2½ x 1½ 2½ x 2½ 2½ x 1½ 2½ x 1½ 1½x1½ 1½x1½

1½x1½ 1½x1½ 1½ x 2½ 1½ x 3½ 1½x1½

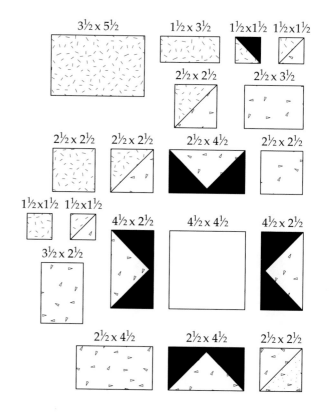

3½ x 5½ 1½ x 3½ 1½x1½ 1½x1½

2½ x 2½ 2½ x 3½

2½ x 2½ 2½ x 2½ 2½ x 4½ 2½ x 2½

1½x1½ 1½x1½ 4½ x 2½ 4½ x 4½ 4½ x 2½

3½ x 2½

2½ x 4½ 2½ x 4½ 2½ x 2½

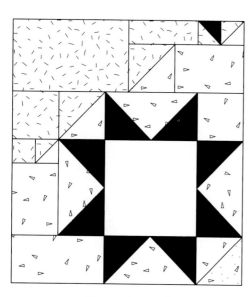

Section 2

Tablerunner #1

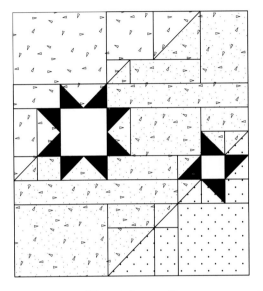

Section 3

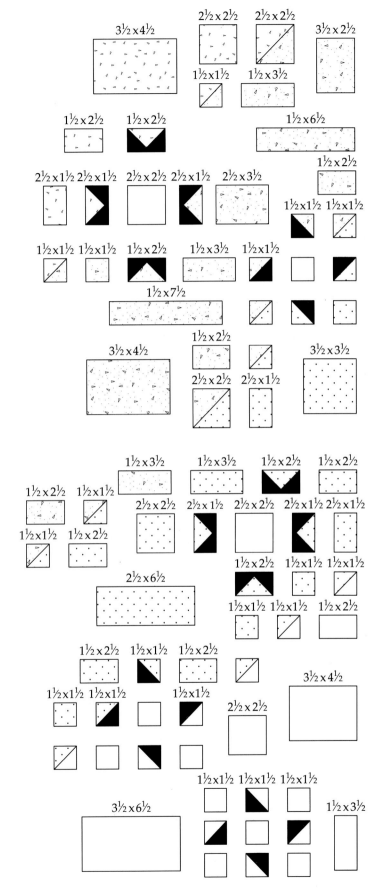

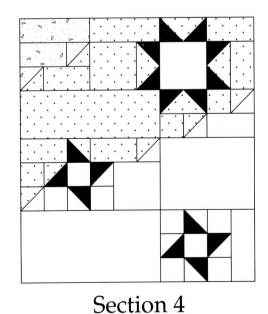

Section 4

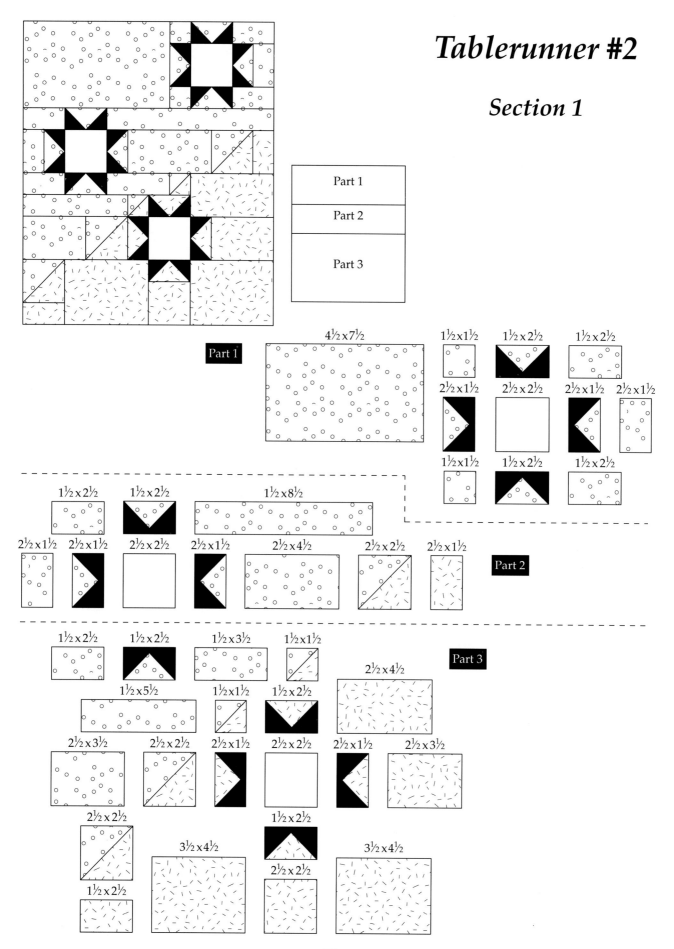

Tablerunner #2

Section 1

| Part 1 |
| Part 2 |
| Part 3 |

Part 1

$4\frac{1}{2}$ x $7\frac{1}{2}$

$1\frac{1}{2}$x$1\frac{1}{2}$ $1\frac{1}{2}$ x $2\frac{1}{2}$ $1\frac{1}{2}$ x $2\frac{1}{2}$

$2\frac{1}{2}$ x $1\frac{1}{2}$ $2\frac{1}{2}$ x $2\frac{1}{2}$ $2\frac{1}{2}$ x $1\frac{1}{2}$ $2\frac{1}{2}$ x $1\frac{1}{2}$

$1\frac{1}{2}$x$1\frac{1}{2}$ $1\frac{1}{2}$ x $2\frac{1}{2}$ $1\frac{1}{2}$ x $2\frac{1}{2}$

$1\frac{1}{2}$ x $2\frac{1}{2}$ $1\frac{1}{2}$ x $2\frac{1}{2}$ $1\frac{1}{2}$x$8\frac{1}{2}$

$2\frac{1}{2}$ x $1\frac{1}{2}$ $2\frac{1}{2}$ x $1\frac{1}{2}$ $2\frac{1}{2}$ x $2\frac{1}{2}$ $2\frac{1}{2}$ x $1\frac{1}{2}$ $2\frac{1}{2}$ x $4\frac{1}{2}$ $2\frac{1}{2}$ x $2\frac{1}{2}$ $2\frac{1}{2}$ x $1\frac{1}{2}$

Part 2

Part 3

$1\frac{1}{2}$ x $2\frac{1}{2}$ $1\frac{1}{2}$ x $2\frac{1}{2}$ $1\frac{1}{2}$ x $3\frac{1}{2}$ $1\frac{1}{2}$x$1\frac{1}{2}$

$1\frac{1}{2}$ x $5\frac{1}{2}$ $1\frac{1}{2}$x$1\frac{1}{2}$ $1\frac{1}{2}$ x $2\frac{1}{2}$ $2\frac{1}{2}$ x $4\frac{1}{2}$

$2\frac{1}{2}$ x $3\frac{1}{2}$ $2\frac{1}{2}$ x $2\frac{1}{2}$ $2\frac{1}{2}$ x $1\frac{1}{2}$ $2\frac{1}{2}$ x $2\frac{1}{2}$ $2\frac{1}{2}$ x $1\frac{1}{2}$ $2\frac{1}{2}$ x $3\frac{1}{2}$

$2\frac{1}{2}$ x $2\frac{1}{2}$ $1\frac{1}{2}$ x $2\frac{1}{2}$

$3\frac{1}{2}$ x $4\frac{1}{2}$ $3\frac{1}{2}$ x $4\frac{1}{2}$

$2\frac{1}{2}$ x $2\frac{1}{2}$

$1\frac{1}{2}$ x $2\frac{1}{2}$

Tablerunner #2

Section 2

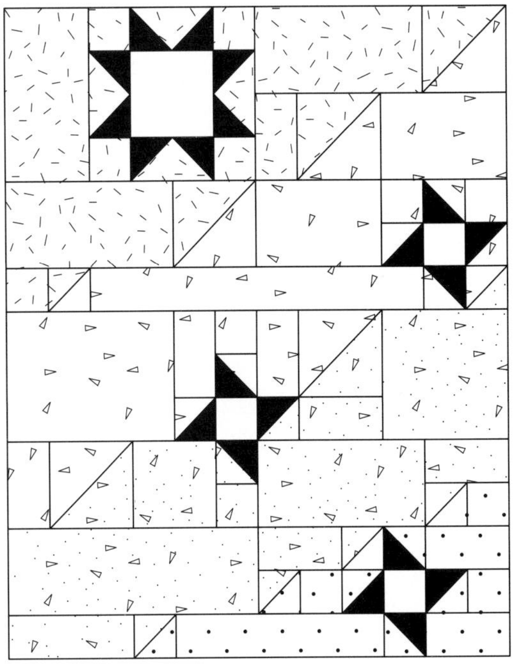

Part 1

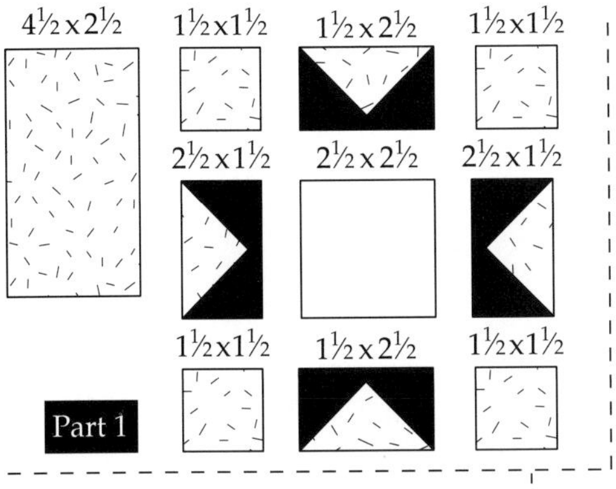

4½ x 2½	1½ x 1½	1½ x 2½	1½ x 1½
	2½ x 1½	2½ x 2½	2½ x 1½
	1½ x 1½	1½ x 2½	1½ x 1½

Part 2

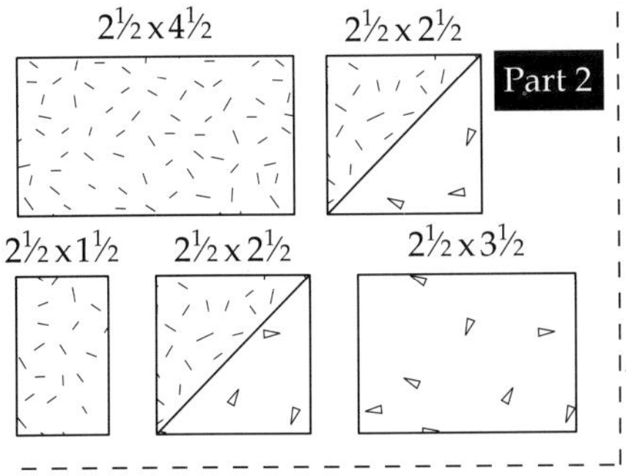

2½ x 4½	2½ x 2½
2½ x 1½	2½ x 2½	2½ x 3½

Part 3

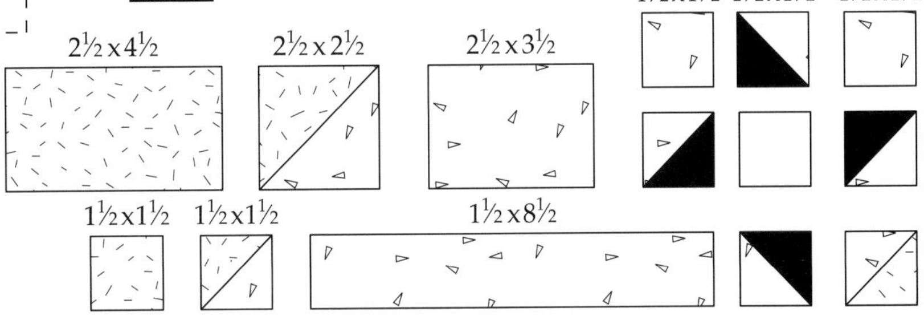

Part 1	Part 2
Part 3	
Part 4	
Part 5	

2½ x 4½	2½ x 2½	2½ x 3½	1½ x 1½	1½ x 1½	1½ x 1½
1½ x 1½	1½ x 1½	1½ x 8½			

Part 4

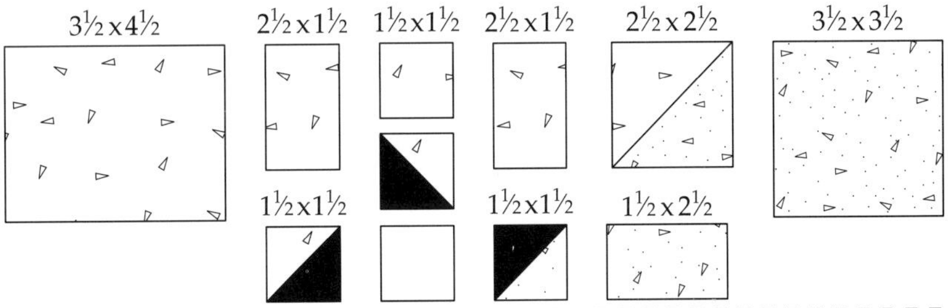

3½ x 4½	2½ x 1½	1½ x 1½	2½ x 1½	2½ x 2½	3½ x 3½
	1½ x 1½	1½ x 1½	1½ x 2½		

Part 5

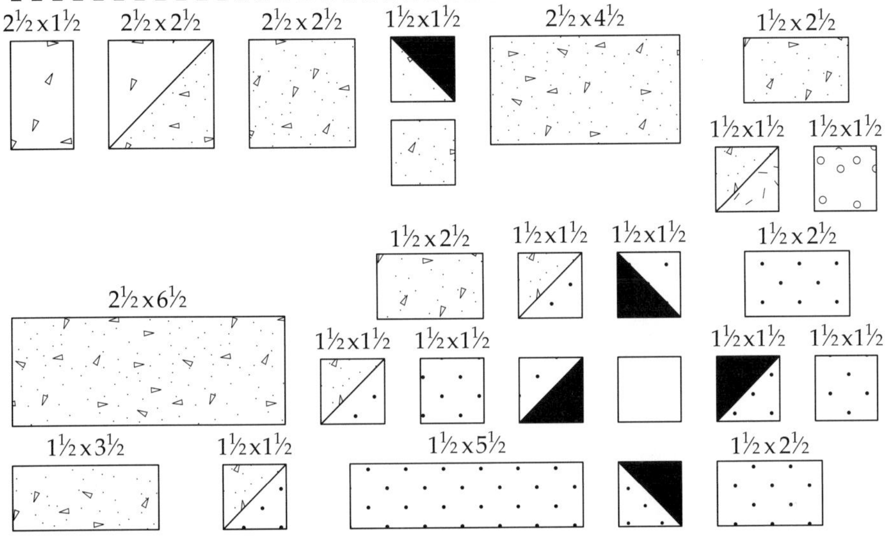

2½ x 1½	2½ x 2½	2½ x 2½	1½ x 1½	2½ x 4½	1½ x 2½

1½ x 1½   1½ x 1½

2½ x 6½	1½ x 2½	1½ x 1½	1½ x 1½	1½ x 2½
	1½ x 1½	1½ x 1½		1½ x 1½	1½ x 1½

1½ x 3½	1½ x 1½	1½ x 5½	1½ x 2½

89

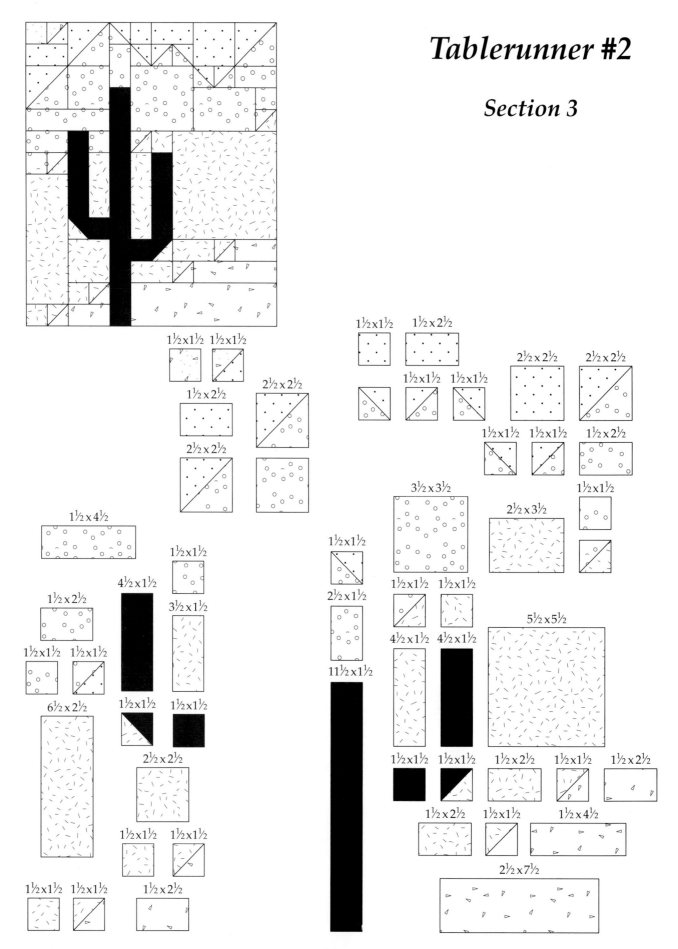

Tablerunner #2

Section 4

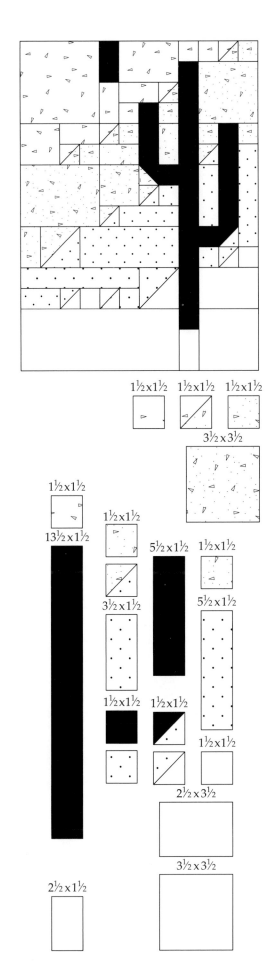

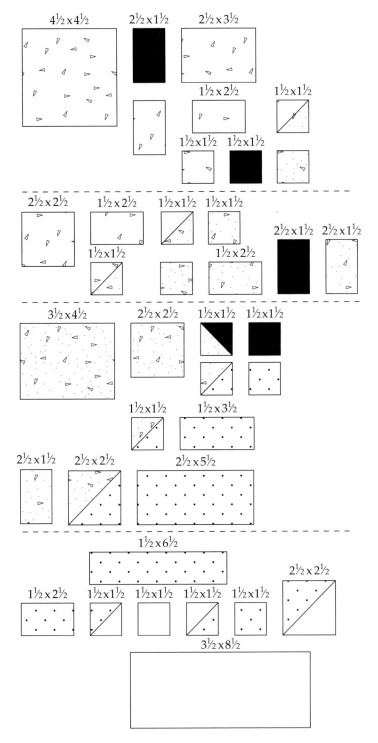

$4\frac{1}{2} \times 4\frac{1}{2}$
$2\frac{1}{2} \times 1\frac{1}{2}$
$2\frac{1}{2} \times 3\frac{1}{2}$
$1\frac{1}{2} \times 2\frac{1}{2}$
$1\frac{1}{2} \times 1\frac{1}{2}$
$1\frac{1}{2} \times 1\frac{1}{2}$
$1\frac{1}{2} \times 1\frac{1}{2}$

$2\frac{1}{2} \times 2\frac{1}{2}$
$1\frac{1}{2} \times 2\frac{1}{2}$
$1\frac{1}{2} \times 1\frac{1}{2}$
$1\frac{1}{2} \times 1\frac{1}{2}$
$1\frac{1}{2} \times 1\frac{1}{2}$
$1\frac{1}{2} \times 2\frac{1}{2}$
$2\frac{1}{2} \times 1\frac{1}{2}$
$2\frac{1}{2} \times 1\frac{1}{2}$

$3\frac{1}{2} \times 4\frac{1}{2}$
$2\frac{1}{2} \times 2\frac{1}{2}$
$1\frac{1}{2} \times 1\frac{1}{2}$
$1\frac{1}{2} \times 1\frac{1}{2}$
$1\frac{1}{2} \times 1\frac{1}{2}$
$1\frac{1}{2} \times 3\frac{1}{2}$

$2\frac{1}{2} \times 1\frac{1}{2}$
$2\frac{1}{2} \times 2\frac{1}{2}$
$2\frac{1}{2} \times 5\frac{1}{2}$

$1\frac{1}{2} \times 6\frac{1}{2}$
$2\frac{1}{2} \times 2\frac{1}{2}$
$1\frac{1}{2} \times 2\frac{1}{2}$
$1\frac{1}{2} \times 1\frac{1}{2}$
$1\frac{1}{2} \times 1\frac{1}{2}$
$1\frac{1}{2} \times 1\frac{1}{2}$
$1\frac{1}{2} \times 1\frac{1}{2}$

$3\frac{1}{2} \times 8\frac{1}{2}$

$1\frac{1}{2} \times 1\frac{1}{2}$
$1\frac{1}{2} \times 1\frac{1}{2}$
$1\frac{1}{2} \times 1\frac{1}{2}$
$3\frac{1}{2} \times 3\frac{1}{2}$

$1\frac{1}{2} \times 1\frac{1}{2}$
$1\frac{1}{2} \times 1\frac{1}{2}$
$5\frac{1}{2} \times 1\frac{1}{2}$
$1\frac{1}{2} \times 1\frac{1}{2}$

$13\frac{1}{2} \times 1\frac{1}{2}$
$3\frac{1}{2} \times 1\frac{1}{2}$
$5\frac{1}{2} \times 1\frac{1}{2}$

$1\frac{1}{2} \times 1\frac{1}{2}$
$1\frac{1}{2} \times 1\frac{1}{2}$

$1\frac{1}{2} \times 1\frac{1}{2}$

$2\frac{1}{2} \times 3\frac{1}{2}$

$3\frac{1}{2} \times 3\frac{1}{2}$

$2\frac{1}{2} \times 1\frac{1}{2}$

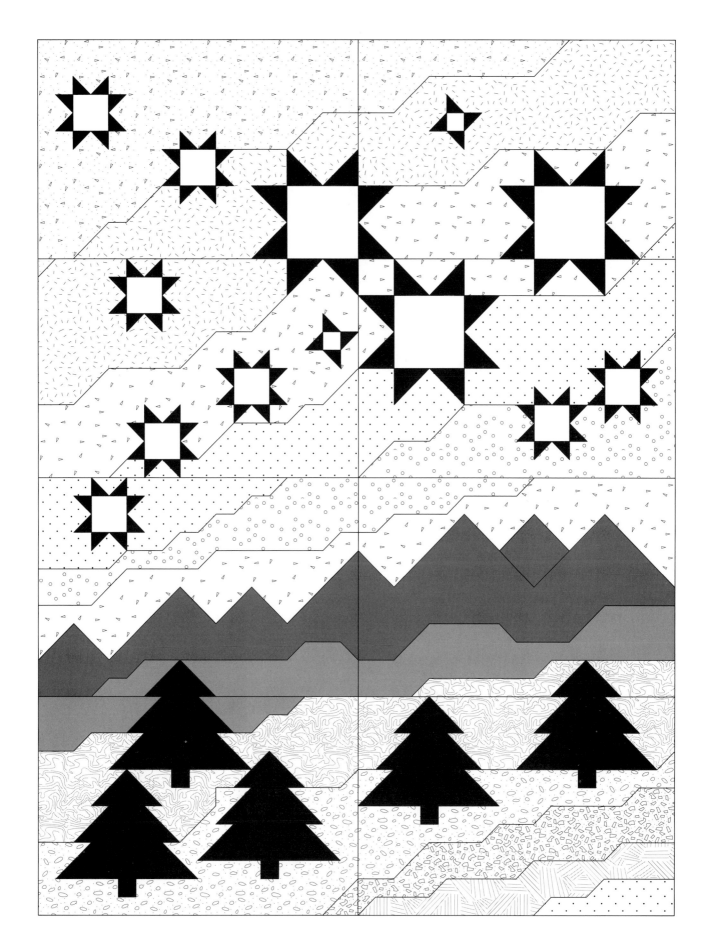